ETIENNE DECROUX

Routledge Performance Practitioners is a series of introductory guides to the key theatre-makers of the last century. Each volume explains the background to and the work of one of the major influences on twentieth- and twenty-first-century performance.

These compact, well-illustrated and clearly written books will unravel the contribution of modern theatre's most charismatic innovators. *Etienne Decroux* is the first book to combine:

- an overview of Decroux's life and work
- an analysis of Decroux's *Words on Mime*, the first book to be written about this art
- a series of practical exercises offering an introduction to corporeal mime technique.

As a first step toward critical understanding, and as an initial exploration before going on to further primary research, **Routledge Performance Practitioners** are unbeatable value for today's student.

Thomas Leabhart is Professor of Theatre and Resident Artist at Pomona College, California. He edits *Mime Journal*, performs and teaches internationally, and is a member of the Artistic Staff of Eugenio Barba's ISTA (International School of Theatre Anthropology).

ROUTLEDGE PERFORMANCE PRACTITIONERS

Series editor: Franc Chamberlain, University College Cork

Routledge Performance Practitioners is an innovative series of introductory handbooks on key figures in twentieth- and twenty-first-century performance practice. Each volume focuses on a theatre-maker whose practical and theoretical work has in some way transformed the way we understand theatre and performance. The books are carefully structured to enable the reader to gain a good grasp of the fundamental elements underpinning each practitioner's work. They will provide an inspiring springboard for future study, unpacking and explaining what can initially seem daunting.

The main sections of each book cover:

* personal biography
* explanation of key writings
* description of significant productions
* reproduction of practical exercises.

Volumes currently available in the series are:

Eugenio Barba by Jane Turner
Augusto Boal by Frances Babbage
Michael Chekhov by Franc Chamberlain
Jacques Copeau by Mark Evans
Etienne Decroux by Thomas Leabhart
Jerzy Grotowski by James Slowiak and Jairo Cuesta
Anna Halprin by Libby Worth and Helen Poyner
Jacques Lecoq by Simon Murray
Joan Littlewood by Nadine Holdsworth
Vsevolod Meyerhold by Jonathan Pitches
Ariane Mnouchkine by Judith Miller
Konstantin Stanislavsky by Bella Merlin
Hijikata Tatsumi and Ohno Kazuo by Sondra Horton Fraleigh
    and Tamah Nakamura
Robert Wilson by Maria Shevtsova

Frontispiece Etienne Decroux in his study, 1953. Photograph: E. B. Weill

Future volumes will include:

Antonin Artaud
Pina Bausch
Bertolt Brecht
Peter Brook
Rudolf Laban
Robert Lepage
Lee Strasberg
Mary Wigman

ETIENNE DECROUX

Thomas Leabhart

Routledge
Taylor & Francis Group

LONDON AND NEW YORK

First published 2007
by Routledge
2 Park Square, Milton Park, Abingdon, Oxon OX14 4RN

Simultaneously published in the USA and Canada
by Routledge

711 Third Avenue, New York, NY 10017
Routledge is an imprint of the Taylor & Francis Group, an informa business

© 2007 Thomas Leabhart

Typeset in Perpetua by
Newgen Imaging Systems (P) Ltd., Chennai, India

British Library Cataloguing in Publication Data
A catalogue record for this book is available from
the British Library

Library of Congress Cataloging in Publication Data
Leabhart, Thomas.
    Etienne Decroux / by Thomas Leabhart.
      p. cm. – (Routledge performance practitioners)
    Includes bibliographical references and index.
    1. Decroux, Etienne, 1898–1991. 2. Mimes – France –
Biography. 3. Mime. I. Title
PN1986.D43L43 2007
792.302'8092–dc22   2006033864

ISBN13: 978–0–415–35436–3 (hbk)
ISBN13: 978–0–415–35437–0 (pbk)
ISBN13: 978–0–203–00102–8 (ebk)

FOR SALLY

CONTENTS

List of plates   xi
List of figures   xiii
Acknowledgments   xv

1   A PROMETHEAN LIFE   1

    Introduction   1
    The life of Etienne Decroux   2
    Chez Copeau: The Chapel, the laboratory, the school   6
    Jean-Louis Barrault   10
    1789 and *The Extravagant Captain Smith*   11
    Children of Paradise   12
    Marcel Marceau   13
    Performance at La Maison de la Chimie   14
    New York years   18
    Last years in Boulogne-Billancourt   18
    Decroux's "underground" school   19
    What Decroux accomplished   22
    Decroux and Asian theatre   26
    Decroux and Grotowski   27
    The vibrato and dynamic immobility in Decroux's work   31
    Transmission: patience is a long passion   34
    Transmission of what?   35

"If Corporeal Mime survives, the world will survive" 35
The great project 37
Notes 38

2 **SUMMARY AND ANALYSIS OF *WORDS ON MIME*** 39
Chapter 1: sources 40
Chapter 2: theatre and mime 55
Chapter 3: dance and mime 60
Chapter 4: mime and mime 63
Note 72

3 **DECROUX AS DIRECTOR/CREATOR : HOW
DID DECROUX MAKE A PERFORMANCE?** 73
Banishing text 73
Making performances from improvisation 74
Decroux's actor 76
Funding for performances 77
The other "alien arts" 78
The movement itself: counterweights 79
The dynamic construction – "dynamo-rhythm" 81
Material actions suggest mental states 83
The Carpenter 84
The Washerwoman 96
Summary 106

4 **CORPOREAL MIME TECHNIQUE: PRACTICAL
EXERCISES WITH IMMEDIATE APPLICATIONS** 113
Inclinations on a lateral plane 116
Contradictions on a lateral plane 120
Segmented movement, lateral scale,
cumulatively curved 123
Pulling an extensor 124
Double, triple, and quadruple designs 132
Stages of consciousness 133
Movement research: how to create a
"movement score" 134

Bibliography 139
Index 143

PLATES

Frontispiece Etienne Decroux in his study, 1953
1.1 Etienne Decroux, 1953   4
1.2 Charles Deburau, 1853   5
1.3 Etienne Decroux ca. 1959 breaks a long
     moment of dynamic immobility in his
     midnight lecture demonstration at the
     Morosco Theatre in New York City   33
2.1 Etienne Decroux ca. 1959 improvises with a
     cane in his midnight lecture demonstration
     at the Morosco Theatre in New York City   41
2.2 Etienne Decroux ca. 1959 emphasizes a point
     during rehearsals in New York City   61
3.1 Etienne Decroux in *The Carpenter* ca. 1950.
     Here the Carpenter holds the screwdriver
     aloft prior to placing it in the tool box. Note
     the wrists resisting the forearms, and the
     arms resisting the shoulders, to create an
     energetic design based on opposition   87
3.2 Steven Wasson in *The Carpenter*, 1994.
     Wasson studied with Decroux from
     1980 to 1984, and served as his teaching
     assistant. With Corinne Soum he directs

the Théâtre de l'Ange Fou and a corporeal
mime school in London   88

3.3 Thomas Leabhart in *The Carpenter*, 1974.
Here the Carpenter, in a costume designed
by Decroux, draws a figure eight on a
piece of wood   95

3.4 Thomas Leabhart in *The Washerwoman*, 1976.
Decroux changed the name of the piece from
The Washing to *The Washerwoman* in 1973 when
he added this all-white costume – hood, mask,
gloves, and dress   97

3.5 Corinne Soum in *The Washerwoman*, 1994. Soum,
who studied with Decroux from 1978 to 1984, also
served as his teaching assistant. With Steven
Wasson, she directs the Théâtre de l'Ange
Fou and a corporeal mime school in London   105

3.6 (a)–(d) Marise Flash in *The Washing*, 2006. Flash,
who worked with Decroux from 1949–55, has taught
movement for actors, mime and improvisation,
at the Piccolo Teatro in Milan since 1954   107

4.1 Etienne Decroux and Thomas Leabhart in the
basement school in Boulogne-Billancourt,
1970. The window to the right opens out to the
garden; white curtains close across the end of
the room to create a more theatrical space for
improvisations   114

4.2 Madame and Monsieur Decroux in their kitchen
in Boulogne-Billancourt, 1975. Decroux, dressed
in his usual black boxing shorts and long-sleeved
shirt, waits by the door to shake each student's
hand at the end of the class   136

4.3 Etienne Decroux in his basement studio, 1975.
This photograph captures the playful and
whimsical aspects of Decroux's personality   137

FIGURES

4.1	Decroux articulates the human body	115
4.2–4.5	The lateral scale	117
4.6–4.9	The lateral scale	118
4.10	Head inclination	119
4.11	Head translation	119
4.12	Head rotation	119
4.13–4.15	Contradictions on a lateral plane	121
4.16–4.19	Contradictions on a lateral plane	122
4.20	Segmented curve on a lateral plane	123
4.21–24	The extensor	125
4.25–28	The extensor	127
4.29–32	The extensor	128
4.33–36	The extensor	129
4.37–39	The extensor	130

ACKNOWLEDGMENTS

I owe inestimable debts of gratitude to Etienne Decroux and his wife Suzanne (née Lodieu) Decroux who nurtured my interest in Corporeal Mime from 1968 through 1972, and to a lesser degree after I left the school until Decroux's passing in 1991; my (then) classmates and now my colleagues in the Decroux movement around the world; my students for more than thirty years; and especially to Maximilien Decroux for his generosity in allowing me to cite from his father's published and unpublished works.

Decroux often said that one could not select one's genetic line, but that one could select one's artistic family. I thank this unique artistic family which continues to nurture and stimulate my work.

I extend my deep gratitude to Madame Etienne Bertrand Weill for allowing us to publish the photographs of Decroux taken by her late husband on pp. ii and 4; to Ben Acland and Kate Goodwillie for the line drawings for Chapter 4, and to the Pomona College Faculty Research Committee for support in their preparation; to my editor Franc Chamberlain for his sound advice and support; to Ben Acland for patiently and efficiently coordinating details and reading and commenting on drafts; and especially to Sally Leabhart for translation, editorial work, and thirty-five years of partnership.

A PROMETHEAN LIFE

INTRODUCTION

From my daily work with him over a four-year period, and subsequent visits over more than a decade, I know of Etienne Decroux's deep and abiding conviction for what he called the Cathedral of Corporeal Mime, a project he imagined would consume the lifetime of many workers; I know too that he pursued his mission determinedly and single-mindedly. As one who believed his sincerity, and not an impartial observer (if such a thing could exist), in this book I have told, in the measure possible, Decroux's story as I think he would have wanted it told. With the same information, a different writer could tell the story of a misfit and sometimes a buffoon, a megalomaniac, a man with typically nineteenth-century French views of women, and one who alienated many.

Having known Decroux and his penchants – his taste and his temperament – I surmise he would have chosen tragedy as the genre for the story of his life, rather than melodrama, farce, or theatre of the absurd. Yet, in this story of a Promethean "man who preferred to stand," we glimpse an agile, masked, and cavorting Commedia dell' arte actor (but never a pantomime!) skittering around the edges of these otherwise serious pages. See Plate 4.3.

Decroux's appearance in the Performance Practitioners Series places him accurately in a line of important twentieth-century theatre reformers, rescuing him from years of oblivion and benign neglect.

When I mentioned to Italian theatre historian Nicola Savarese that Decroux had died in 1991, he replied with astonishment: "In theatre history terms, the body is not yet cold in the grave!" Truly one might say that the body of Decroux's work lives on vibrantly today through his students and their students in schools including those in London, Paris, Rome, Naples, Montreal, Vancouver, Barcelona, and Southern California. Graduate students in Italy, France, and Spain regularly select areas of Decroux's work as thesis or dissertation topics. In addition to this book, a large and important volume entitled *Etienne Decroux, mime corporel: textes, études et témoignages* (Etienne Decroux, corporeal mime: texts, studies and first-hand accounts) appeared in France in 2003, and Routledge has scheduled a *Decroux Companion* for publication in the near future. These strong indicators suggest that Decroux will not remain an idiosyncratically colorful footnote to theatre history, but, with the passing years, increasingly take his place among major twentieth-century theatre reformers.

THE LIFE OF ETIENNE DECROUX

CHILDHOOD

Etienne Decroux's father, Marie-Edouard, a mason, walked from his native Haute Savoie to Paris, where he married the cook in a household which had employed him as *maître d'hôtel* (Benheïm 2003: 241). Decroux, born July 19, 1898, spoke affectionately of both parents but saw his father as the decisive figure in his early life. He not only built houses, but also cooked meals, bathed him, cared for him when he was ill, cut his hair, and for many years took him every Monday to the *café-concert*, a kind of music hall. With his voice, he "caress[ed] the heart" of his disappointed son, found secretly crying after the departure of the first circus he had ever seen. He took his son on visits to a family of Italian sculptors and "incited me to prolonged conversations on justice and injustice. In our neighborhood, he was the only person thinking as he did"; he "read verse to me in a restrained manner . . . . I looked at my father as one looks at a moving statue" (Decroux 1950: 2). Later he wrote: "Thanks to him, for me, there is nothing higher than a political sense. I have . . . remained impressed with what one could call political lyricism" (Decroux 2003: 57).

An apprentice butcher at thirteen, Decroux subsequently worked as a dishwasher, painter, plumber, mason, roofer, day laborer, dock worker, farm worker, and in a factory repairing wagons; he placed hermetic seals on iceboxes; he was a nurse. In 1920, after three years of military service, Decroux saw Georges Carpentier become the boxing champion of the world, combining a strength and grace that would influence Decroux's subsequent endeavors: "In sport I saw the origin of dramatic art. I had for it an almost dazed admiration" (Decroux 1950: 3). He later explained, "These things, seen and experienced first hand, gradually moved into the back of my mind, down the back of my arms, and finally down to my fingertips where they modified the fingerprints" (Decroux 1985: ii).

In the first years of Decroux's life, we see themes that he developed throughout his career. In his love of the circus, we see his penchant for energetic and highly trained actors on an empty stage. Decroux's early reverence for sculpture and his vision of his father as a "moving statue" adumbrate mobile statuary which became one of the categories of Decroux's Corporeal Mime technique. At the *café-concert* Decroux saw the last gasps of nineteenth-century pantomime, the only art he frankly "detested," and from which his technique radically departed. Whereas pantomime primarily emphasizes the body's extremities and surfaces while depicting charming and entertaining vignettes, Corporeal Mime movements begin in the deepest parts of the body (inside the biceps and the buttocks, and from the abdomen below the navel), and do not primarily aim at entertainment (see Table 1.1 and Plates 1.1 and 1.2). According to Eugenio Barba, Corporeal Mime encompasses a

Table 1.1 A comparison of Corporeal Mime and Pantomime

Corporeal Mime (Etienne Decroux)	Pantomime (Charles Deburau)
Twentieth-century modernist	Nineteenth-century romantic
Emphasis on articulated trunk	Emphasis on expressive face and hands
Body uncovered, face masked	Body covered, face exposed
Nonnarrative (symbolic or abstract)	Storytelling (linear)
Physical causality replaces plot	Traditional beginning, middle, end
Gestures exist for themselves	Gestures replace words
Often tragic	Often comic
Lower center of gravity	Higher center of gravity

Plate 1.1 Etienne Decroux, 1953. Photograph: E. B. Weill

Plate 1.2 Charles Deburau, 1853. Photograph: Nadar

"knowledge of the actor's pre-expressive level, how to build up presence, and how to articulate the transformation of energy, [that] is unequaled in Western theatre history" (Barba 1997: 12).

CHEZ COPEAU: THE CHAPEL, THE LABORATORY, THE SCHOOL

At twenty-five, Decroux had saved enough money to live a year without working. Having spent a decade as a manual laborer, he wanted a comparatively less physically exhausting life, and imagined that acting would give him time to pursue political interests. In the political world, as in the theatre, his pronounced working-class accent needed correcting; and, in an age without electronic amplification, he had to learn articulation and projection. Decroux entered Jacques Copeau's school to study voice, but instead discovered the body. Copeau, Decroux's first teacher, cultivated the germ of what Decroux would develop, over the course of his career, into Corporeal Mime.

"GIVE ME A BARE STAGE!"

Jacques Copeau (1879–1949), born to a family of manufacturers and sales people, worked as a writer, editor, and critic. In 1913, at age thirty-three, never having set foot on stage, he founded (with actors Charles Dullin, Blanche Albane, Suzanne Bing, and Louis Jouvet) the Théâtre du Vieux Colombier.

Copeau modeled his theatre's stage after historical performance spaces he admired: the Greek theatre, the Commedia dell'arte platform, the Noh stage, the Elizabethan "Wooden O," and the circus ring. All had an open, uncluttered performing area, unfashionable when Copeau leased and renovated the space that became the Théâtre du Vieux Colombier prior to World War I.

Actors to fill such spaces proved more difficult to find. Copeau wrote: "On an empty stage I see how important the actor becomes. His stature, his acting, his *quality*" (Copeau 2000: 182). Copeau required a school to train the actors with quality, but initially was too busy to found one.

As most of his actors were conscripted in World War I, Copeau closed the theatre. Himself unable to serve because of illness, he visited **Edward Gordon Craig** (1872–1966), Emile Jaques-Dalcroze

Edward Gordon Craig (1872–1966), the son of actress Ellen Terry and architect Edward William Godwin, acted (with his mother) in Henry Irving's company at the Lyceum Theatre in London from 1885–97. In the early 1900s he renounced acting, developing instead his career as a stage and costume designer, theoretician, and printmaker. Devising his own revolutionary approach to moveable architectural staging, in 1911 he published *On the Art of the Theatre*.

Editor of *The Mask* (1908–1929), in which he published his famous essay on the Super-Marionette, Craig wanted to abolish Victorian trappings of realism and sentimentality, and to replace them with a more open and symbolic space (influenced by Greek theatre and the open Commedia dell'arte stage). Copeau and Decroux learned important lessons from Craig, who admired Asian theatre forms and advocated total theatre incorporating symbolist set designs, masks, verse, and dance.

(1865–1950), and Adolphe Appia (1862–1928) to focus his thinking about a school. These visits confirmed Copeau's initial intuitions that movement and improvisation must take a central part in training new actors.

Craig influenced Copeau to include theatre crafts, Commedia dell'arte, and Asian theatre forms in his school. Seeing masks and recognizing their importance in Commedia and many Asian forms sparked Copeau's interest in using them as a tool for actor training and, to a more limited degree, in performance (Leigh 1979: 12).

At first, guardedly enthusiastic about Dalcroze's rhythmic gymnastics – called eurhythmics – Copeau imagined incorporating them, with modifications, directly into his school; later he found the gymnastics of **Lt. Hébert** more appropriate since they dealt with lifting real weights, traversing real obstacles, and working in a way more conducive to actors' behavior in response to the real world, rather than in response to musical accompaniment. More lasting influences on Copeau came from Dalcroze's exercises in which students evolved from silence and immobility to movement, sound, and finally words.

Navy Lieutenant Georges Hébert (1875–1957) observed harmonious human bodies accomplishing natural movements necessary to life at sea and on land. For the less industrialized people he - visited, as well as for sailors in the masts and rigging of sailing ships, throwing, running, jumping, carrying, swimming, and so on were essential activities. Hébert advocated working outdoors as lightly clothed as possible, following one's own rhythm of work, according to individual abilities; working with natural obstacles (rocks, logs, uneven terrain), using natural and useful gestures (carrying, pushing, pulling); balancing on one foot, walking on hands and feet; sustained effort to develop endurance and breath, but with an alternation of contrary efforts. His work opposed competitive athletics that was practiced in stadiums to entertain and to break records.

This progression, adopted by Copeau, later permeated Decroux's work (Leigh 1979: 13).

An observation in Copeau's notebook tells us a great deal, not only about Copeau's work, but also about Decroux's later accomplishments:

> I have already noticed, especially with Dalcroze, that the student, as soon as you call upon an emotion (fatigue, joy, sadness, etc.) to provoke a movement, . . . right away, and perhaps unconsciously, out of necessity, he allows the intellectual element to predominate in his action, facial expression. This is an open door to literature and to ham acting.

(Copeau 2000: 101)

Copeau's repression of facial expression in favor of larger physical movement became an important plank in Decroux's theatrical platform. Suzanne Bing, one of Copeau's leading actors and the head of his school, noticed another failing in Dalcroze's work: the rhythmic gymnastics did not allow improvisers to listen to an internal music (impulses), but predicated a conditioned response to external music (Copeau 2000: 114). Hearing and responding to internal impulses, important to Copeau, would constitute the basis of Decroux's work in improvisation and creation.

Copeau spent the remainder of the war years in New York, directing a theatre that advanced the French propaganda effort. During this time, Copeau amplified his ideas on actor training, and specified that craftsmen and carpenters

> use an economy of gesture so that everything seems in its rightful place. That comes from their really doing something, that they do what they do and do it well, knowing the reason, absorbing themselves in it.
>
> (Copeau in Leigh 1979: 19)

Copeau thereby found "a point of departure" for all movement, "a kind of purity of integrity of the individual, a state of calm, of naturalness, of relaxation" (Copeau in Leigh 1979: 19), which in turn became central to Decroux's work.

Copeau's theatre reopened in Paris in February 1920, as he increasingly referred to the school and theatre as laboratories. In 1921, the school reopened, engaging a staff to assist Copeau, Bing, Jouvet, and Copeau's daughter, Marie-Hélène.

COPEAU'S NEW CHAPTER

In spring of 1924, Copeau experienced a crisis provoked by dissention among his supporters, glimmers of brilliance in the school work, accumulated fatigue, the theatre's constant financial problems, and his recent conversion to Catholicism. Closing the Vieux-Colombier, he retreated without funding to a chateau near Beaune, accompanied by students and colleagues. Decroux joined them in October 1924, but left in February 1925, along with ten others, as the financially uncertain venture slowly unraveled.

AFTER COPEAU: "THOSE OF US WHO LEFT TOOK FIRE WITH US"

After leaving Copeau's retreat, Decroux returned to Paris where, after acting briefly with Gaston Baty (1885–1952) and Louis Jouvet (1887–1951), he spent eight consecutive years with Charles Dullin (1885–1949). Concurrently, Decroux frequented the anarchist milieu until 1929. There he met his wife-to-be, Suzanne Lodieu, also a political militant who worked as a shoemaker's apprentice; they married in 1930. In 1931,

Jean-Gaspard Deburau (1796–1846), born into an itinerant French circus family in Bohemia, performed with his family in a tent. Tightrope walker, trapeze artist, acrobat, juggler, magician, and most notably pantomime at the Théâtre des Funambles, where as Baptiste – his own refashioning of Pierrot – he was for years spectacularly popular. The film *Children of Paradise* recounts his life.

the newly married Decrouxs performed *Primitive Life* in the Salle Lancry in Paris (Lorelle 1974: 107); the same year, Decroux formed his own theatre troupe, A Seed, to which he devoted seven years. This anticapitalist and anti-Stanislavskian group produced movement and choral works for Leftist organizations, but never for communist groups (Benheïm 2003: 247).

JEAN-LOUIS BARRAULT

In 1931, twenty-year-old Jean-Louis Barrault began studying at Charles Dullin's Théâtre de l'Atelier where he met Decroux, then a member of Dullin's troupe. Barrault remembers Decroux as an eccentric who stylized his roles to the point of dancing them, and whose friends spoke of him with a little sidelong smile. Decroux, at that time a "puritan revolutionary" who "cultivated the more-than-perfect" (Barrault 1951: 21, 23), solicited people to continue the corporeal work he had begun at the Vieux Colombier. Decroux won over Barrault who became his first disciple and his collaborator.

Vegetarians and nudists, bouncing off the walls of the Atelier basement while the other actors played cards or drank, Decroux and Barrault (with Suzanne, Decroux's wife) presented *Medieval Life* at the Atelier in 1931, continuing *Primitive Life*, presented earlier in the year.

After two years of intense collaboration, laying the foundation for modern mime, they performed *Ancient Combat* for Dullin who felt their work reached the technical perfection of Japanese actors. Dullin's Atelier, which embraced theatre as a laboratory, numbered among the few Parisian theatres where experimentation could occur.

Two years of work revealed to Barrault what many students afterward remarked: Decroux's uncompromising passion for art, and his rigorous devotion, usually made long-term collaboration impossible. Barrault went on to become a perennial enfant-terrible, popular movie actor and, with his wife Madeline Renaud, the director of one of Europe's most important theatre companies, la Compagnie Renaud-Barrault.

1789 AND *THE EXTRAVAGANT CAPTAIN SMITH*

Decroux's temperament in teaching extended onto the stage where he stopped less than successful performances, insulting the audience if they laughed inappropriately and uncomprehendingly.

In 1937, A Seed disbanded. Two of his previous company members joined Decroux and his wife to form a new group called 1789, which performed existing repertoire and new mime pieces by Decroux entitled *The Carpenter* and *The Machine*. One critic wrote of them: "While they perform, one believes oneself to be in a laboratory, in a temple, and in a workshop. It is research, it is soul, and it is work" (in Benheïm 2003: 248). In 1938, Decroux performed one hundred times in his dining-room for audiences of two or three. The group 1789 lasted one year; at the outbreak of the war in 1939, Decroux ceased all overtly political activity, Corporeal Mime becoming his political party.

Decroux earned his living from the theatre, and developed Corporeal Mime in his spare time. He played over sixty-five roles in works by Aristophanes, Ruzzante, Shakespeare, Ben Jonson, Molière, Tolstoy, Strindberg, Pirandello, Marcel Achard, and Jules Romains. His directors were, among others, Jacques Copeau, Gaston Baty, Louis Jouvet, Charles Dullin, Antonin Artaud, and Marcel Herrand (Decroux 1985: i). The most commercially successful theatrical work of his prewar career was the eponymous leading role in the play *The Extravagant Captain Smith* in 1938 and 1939 (Benheïm 2003: 250). Decroux also especially enjoyed performing Trotsky in *Tsar Lénine*, and Tchernozium in *le Quadrature du Cercle* (Decroux 1950: 4).

With the declaration of war in 1939, Decroux joined the military service. In 1940, during the dark days of the Occupation, Decroux continued perfecting *The Machine, The Carpenter, The Washing*, and *Character Walks in Place*, performing them another hundred times for audiences of three or four spectators. In 1941, Decroux opened his school and presented his first large composition, *Camping*, for one performance at the Comédie des Champs-Elysées. Decroux presented *Passage of Men Across the Earth* and other pieces ten times in public and one hundred times for invited audiences in his school. In 1942, Decroux gave public performances at the Salon d'Automne and the Théâtre des Ambassadeurs.

During his career, Decroux acted in twenty films, perhaps the best known being *Children of Paradise* (1943), directed by Marcel Carné.

CHILDREN OF PARADISE

In 1943, Jacques Prévert, at Barrault's suggestion, wrote the scenario for a three-hour film based on the life of the nineteenth-century pantomime performer, **Jean-Gaspard Deburau**. Deburau performed silently because of government regulations limiting the number and *genre* of Paris theatres in the 1840s; German occupation forces similarly censored French theatre, making Deburau's story appropriate in 1943–44. Marcel Carné directed the film amid shortages of electricity, costume materials, wood, plaster, and motion-picture film stock. The title, *Children of Paradise*, referenced the name given to the poor who could afford only the cheapest seats far up in the balconies (in the gods). These theatres lined the Boulevard du Temple, called the "Boulevard du Crime" in the time of Louis-Philippe because of the subject matter of their melodramatic plays. Arletty played the central role of Garance, a great beauty whose three suitors were historical figures in 1840 Paris: Deburau (played by Jean-Louis Barrault); Fréderick Lemaître, a melodrama actor (played by Pierre Brasseur); and the killer known to all Paris, Pierre-François Lacenaire (played by Marcel Herrand). Decroux performed the part of Anselme Deburau, Jean-Gaspard's father.

One of the most successful French films of all time, *Children of Paradise* had an impact on the development of twentieth-century mime. It appeared when the new modernist tendencies in mime had taken root only tentatively. While years of professional activity had established Decroux's role as master teacher and innovator, his antipathy to performance and his love of research made him almost invisible. If modern mime were to appear outside Decroux's atelier, a brilliant student would have to bring it out. Barrault's first performances as a mime in a modernist vein had impressed Artaud and garnered critical if not popular success; as Barrault later wrote, "there were so few people who really understood it [modern mime]. Hardly anyone appreciated it then" (Barrault 1951: 29). One can conjecture what would have happened had Barrault subsequently not gone into the speaking theatre, or if *Children of Paradise*, with its seductive images of nostalgic and charming nineteenth-century pantomime, had not so profoundly impressed the public. As it happened (with palpable irony), Decroux and his most famous pupil unintentionally revived nineteenth-century pantomime's popularity, despite having dedicated themselves for years to the evolution of its antithesis: their Corporeal Mime aimed not to recreate a recognizable reality but rather to explore movement possibilities and "pure" drama – drama independent of plot.

In 1944, while *Children of Paradise* was playing to thousands in movie theatres, Decroux and his students gave private showings for 10–50 people in the small hall of the Foyer des Beaux Arts. Also in 1944, while teaching for Dullin at the Théâtre Sarah-Bernhardt, he met a student named Marcel Marceau (Lorelle 1974: 114)

MARCEL MARCEAU

> To us, [Chaplin] was a god. As a boy I sat entranced in motion picture houses, watching those shining images unfold before me. It was then that I determined to become a pantomimist.
>
> (Marceau 1958: 59)

After the war, in which he worked for the Resistance and in which his father perished at Auschwitz, Marcel Mangel became Marcel Marceau and moved to Paris. Taking a job teaching theatre in a children's school in Sèvres, he met Eliane Guyon, then Decroux's student. Marceau studied with Decroux for three years in Dullin's school, going on to become a solo performer of white-faced pantomime. Touring the world to great critical and popular acclaim, he revived single-handedly the art invented by Jean-Gaspard Deburau in the previous century. For half a century, his name was synonymous with mime, imitators performing on street-corners and at birthday parties the world over.

Decroux spoke of Marceau's brilliance with admiration, but also with disappointment because of Marceau's popular and entertaining performance style which owed more to nineteenth-century white-faced pantomime of the kind seen in *The Children of Paradise* than it did to Decroux's abstract, often formalist, demanding, and difficult research. Decroux's work eschewed story-telling and obvious narrative – the life and soul of Marceau's work – in favor of abstraction and evocation.

The divide between them became evident when Marceau performed in New York in the 1950s at a large theatre to sold-out houses while

Decroux lived and taught in the same city, on the Lower East Side in a small walk-up flat. Carlo Mazzone Clementi, Italian Commedia dell'arte actor and teacher, visited Decroux then and reported the following conversation.

CARLO: Etienne did you know that Marceau is performing at City Center?

DECROUX: (after a thoughtful pause during which a little smile played around the corners of his lips) Ah, yes. The Pope is in St. Peter's, and Jesus Christ is still in the catacombs!

This story illustrates Decroux's passionate (quasi-religious) commitment to modern mime, his disdain for anyone (even a brilliant former student) who refused to join his search for the absolute – anyone who was not militant. The word "militant" takes on special importance considering Decroux's background as an anarchist and militant socialist. For Decroux, desire to please an audience, to win them over, revealed a lack of taste, of courage, or even a moral or spiritual failure. He dismissed pantomime, saying: "I detested this form which seemed to me comic even before one knew what it was about" (Decroux 2003: 61).

PERFORMANCE AT LA MAISON DE LA CHIMIE

In 1945 Decroux and Barrault performed *Ancient Combat* as part of *Antony and Cleopatra* at the Comédie Française, an unsuccessful marriage of rich text and rich movement. (Decroux later preached a doctrine of rich text necessitating "poor" movement, and "poor" text requiring rich movement.) The most important mime event of this period, however, occurred not at the Comédie Française, but, on June 27, 1945 at the Maison de la Chimie in Paris, where more than a thousand spectators attended a performance by Decroux, Barrault, Eliane Guyon, Jean Dorcy (master of ceremonies), and Edward Gordon Craig (guest of honor). Describing what took place, Jean Dorcy defines Corporeal Mime:

With corporeal mime, we no longer read known forms, we decode, reassemble, and appreciate according to our knowledge and our emotional state: the passive observer becomes active. Could one dream of a more fecund meeting of actor and audience?

(Dorcy 1945)

Dorcy's use of the word "decode" does not mean that Decroux created guessing-games. To the contrary, Decroux detested that illusionistic play which casts the audience in the role of translator, trying to interpret the performer's signals into verbal equivalents. Instead, Decroux proceeded by analogy and by metaphor: to Decroux's eye, for example, one actor rising up on stage was like all of humanity rising up. This decoding is something quite different, then, from an actor pretending to be carried aloft by a helium balloon and the audience needing to figure out that a hand rising above the head as the actor rises up onto toes means "man being lifted up by helium balloon." Dorcy continues:

> Let us understand that the corporeal mime wants a bare stage, nude actors, and no variation in lighting. For once, the theatre is no longer a cross-roads of all the arts, but the triumph of one art only: that of the body in motion.

(Dorcy 1945)

This love of purity comes from an amalgam of Copeau's and Craig's doctrines taken one step further and identifies Decroux as modernist and formalist, contemporaneous with Dutch Neo-Plasticist painter Piet Mondrian (1872–1944), Romanian abstract sculptor Constantin Brancusi (1876–1957), and others who reduced things to essentials – to a play of form.

According to the program book, the June 27 performance highlighted doctrinal links from Craig to Copeau, from Copeau to Decroux, from Decroux to Barrault, evoking along the way the work of Appia. The program consisted of eight pieces. The first, entitled *Evocation of Concrete Actions*, consisted of three parts: *The Carpenter, The Washing*, and *The Machine*. *The Carpenter* and *The Washing* were simplifications and amplifications of work performed by an individual: in the first, of sawing, planing, hammering, and other actions associated with carpentry; in the second, of washing, rinsing, wringing, hanging out to dry, and mending laundry. Decroux did indeed mean "evocation" rather than "depiction," "reproduction," or "representation." Without the title, an audience might not have any notion that Decroux had begun with these actions, just as an observer of a cubist painting might not identify the subject. Like cubist paintings, these studies resulted from carefully observing the object or action in nature before its sometimes unrecognizable transposition into fragmented and superimposed planes. Just as some twentieth-century music rejected traditional notions of melody, Decroux eschewed apparent narrative apart from the narrative of the actions themselves.

The third part of the opening, *The Machine*, evoked a favored subject for graphic arts, theatre, dance, cinema (Chaplin's *Modern Times*), and mime in these Futurist years; these arts reflected a society radically changed by machines and trying to adjust to them. Decroux daily created and reconstructed mime pieces, many of which, like *The Machine*, had their origin in Copeau's exercises; he created pieces first for himself and his wife, and later with students.

These studies of human and mechanical work preceded *A Counterweight Study*, performed by Decroux's students. Decroux's counterweight exercises carefully analyzed pushing, pulling, carrying, or otherwise displacing objects of varying weights.

Decroux then performed *The Boxer*, *The Wrestler*, *The Bureaucrat*, and *Some Passers-by*. While he probably portrayed the boxer and wrestler in a noble way, concentrating on the dynamics of sports, Decroux's sharp wit and taste for satire doubtless delighted in skewering and deflating affectations in the bureaucrat or the passers-by.

This suite preceded a symbolist mime chorus. Earlier, Decroux had staged speaking choruses for radical socialist and anarchist events. The idea of many voices blending together to articulate a single idea inflamed his imagination. On this occasion, the chorus consisted of only three actors (Decroux, Barrault, and Eliane Guyon) who performed, probably without using their voices, *Passage of Men Across the Earth*. The piece, revived in the 1950s for Decroux's New York company, evokes famine, mass movements of population, revolution, and finally peace. Without story line, or attempt at characterization, it evokes through symbolic collage, in which actors are often masked.

Decroux and Guyon next performed a work-in-progress entitled *Materials for a Biblical Piece*, subtitled *Juxtaposed Figures without Dramatic Connection*. Decroux's aversion to traditional plot-line shows up in every piece, and here in the title is a reminder not to expect it.

Barrault next performed his signature horse-taming sequence, an extract from *About a Mother* (a 1935 adaptation of William Faulkner's *As I Lay Dying*). This came before *Mobile Statuary with Covered Face*, the evening's sublime summit. In this section, Barrault performed *Illness, Suffering, Death* (excerpted from *About a Mother*), and Decroux performed *Differences between Admiration–Adoration–Veneration* "both in the same theme: Will." Decroux placed this purest and most abstract apex of Corporeal Mime just before the crowd-pleasing *Ancient Combat*, which crowned the performance. Decroux's note about the Will signals his self-consciously Promethean approach: he himself, along with the hardest-working of his apprentices, knew the sacrifice of pleasures and comfort required to become proficient in Corporeal Mime.

The evening ended with a lecture on the differences between pantomime and Corporeal Mime. Dorcy found it inappropriate to have such a lecture follow the livelier parts of the program. Decroux the orator, the student of French literature, the politician, felt compelled to provide a commentary, an explication of the "text" the audience had just seen. He had a constant fear that audiences would not understand his work unless he somehow won them over, illuminating his method and also enabling them to see what he saw so clearly.

Craig, reviewing the performance in "At Last a Creator in the Theatre, of the Theatre," places Decroux in the forefront of postwar European work.

> I am tempted to believe that Mr. Decroux possesses genius, but that he is a very suspicious man. He does not dare count on it entirely. He mistrusts it. He prefers to help his genius rather than to possess it and enjoy it. They say he will be seen as the master of mime. I consider that the title already belongs to him.
>
> (Craig 2001: 97)

In 1946, Decroux reprised the role of Captain Smith and, with students, presented *The Factory, The Trees*, and *The Mischevious Spirit* at Théâtre d'Iéna in Paris. Decroux and a small company toured Belgium, Switzerland, Holland, Israel, and England, and performed occasionally in Paris in the following years. During this time he created *Little Soldiers*, *Making Contact*, *Checkers* and *Party*. His school in Paris became more and more popular, and began to draw students from Europe and America.

According to Maximilien Decroux, his father's astringent, unyielding personality made these tours and rehearsals difficult for them. "Etienne Decroux," a colleague wrote, "was hostile to those he was supposed to win over: he disliked his public; and worse still, he had no respect for it. It often seemed as though he took malicious pleasure in antagonizing the audience" (Dorcy 1975: 49).

NEW YORK YEARS

In October of 1957, Decroux began teaching, lecturing, directing, and performing in the United States. After short teaching stints at The Actor's Studio, The Dramatic Workshop, New York University, and The New School, Decroux founded a school in New York, training actors who performed with him at the Kaufmann Concert Hall, Carnegie Hall, and the Cricket Theatre. He also performed solo lecture-demonstrations and taught short workshops at various universities, among them Tufts in Medford, MA and Baylor in Waco, TX. The New York company revived works he had produced before, among them *The Factory, Trees*, certain of Decroux's solos, and a new duet entitled *The Statue*, with Decroux playing the sculptor. Among the solos Decroux performed for largely uncomprehending audiences was his signature piece, *The Carpenter*. (See Chapter 3 for more information on this work.)

LAST YEARS IN BOULOGNE-BILLANCOURT

After five years in New York, Decroux returned to France, living in what had been his father's house in a working-class suburb of Paris, where his school remained until 1986. He continued to "perform" daily in class, but his already fluctuating interest in placing himself or his students before uncomprehending and uninitiated audiences receded. His basement school flourished, attracting students from around the world. Their number varied from as few as six or eight to as many as one hundred in three separate classes each day which he taught with the help of his student-assistants and, at times, his son, Maximilien. He was for some a charismatic teacher; others saw him as a despot, and many saw him as an eccentric man dressed in flannel pajamas, a terry-cloth bath robe and bedroom slippers. He seemed happy, *at home* in every sense of the word, and his teaching blossomed. Suzanne often sang in the kitchen as she cooked; he might shout upstairs to her "They're making progress, you know!" or she would open the door and shout down to him, if she heard his voice take on a threatening tone, "Don't lose your cool, Etienne!" See Plate 4.2. In his teaching he was funny, insulting, witty, charming, angry, brilliant, and prophetic, often in one class. He sang, told jokes, made impossibly difficult puns, and demonstrated exercises that took the breath away, literally and figuratively.

DECROUX'S "UNDERGROUND" SCHOOL

Decroux, like Copeau before him, recognized the school as a precondition to new theatre. But whereas Copeau produced plays successfully with actors who had not studied with him (as literature was their primary component), Decroux found this impossible in Corporeal Mime, where actors could not rely upon literature and had to know a new physical language, taught only by Decroux. He told this joke, about actors who looked right for a role: "You look exactly like a violinist, even if you have never studied music! We are just about to have a concert. Here is the violin, and here is the music. Begin!"

Decroux's underground school, where he formed actors for his new theatre, required him to spend his time in one place, working on himself and his students. Though he left Paris to teach – never as a vacation, until his last years – Decroux more closely resembled Allan de Botton's French "internal traveler" (in *The Art of Travel*) who only traversed the distance from his door to his bed than de Botton's German explorer, an external traveler who mapped the coast of South America. Decroux spent decades closed inside a workroom, carefully articulating the landscape of the body, mapping its expressive articulations, preferring, like the "internal traveler," to work in pajamas and bedroom slippers. He found his workroom in Amsterdam, Tel Aviv, Milan, Stockholm, Zurich, Oslo, Innsbruck, New York, Waco (Texas), and usually in Paris ("Even if I never go out, I like knowing that the Eiffel Tower is there"), but no matter the physical location, he occupied the basement figuratively if not literally, on the margins, invisible to the public eye.

Here are a few (of the many) things that obsessed him during these decades of concentration:

Three ways to move the spine: Bar, chain and accordion describe the three ways Decroux imagined the spine could move.

- Bar indicates the spine moving in straight lines: head, hammer (head and neck together), bust (head, neck, and chest together), etc.
- Chain indicates the spine moving in curved lines as in segmented movements, undulations, compensations, etc.
- Accordion indicates the spine alternately collapsing upon itself and expanding away from the center, like the bellows of an accordion.

Scales: When Decroux said "incline the head without the neck" he discovered his system. From there one can easily say (not always easily do) "now incline the head and the neck – called the hammer – without the chest" and so on, progressing downward through the body (see pp. 117, 118). Making a keyboard of the body, articulating each segment, allows an infinite number of subsequent movements: articulations forward, back, side, in rotation, in rotation on an inclined plane, and in any one of eight triple designs. One can perform a triple design, made of two inclinations and a rotation, with the head, the bust, the trunk, and the Eiffel Tower (the whole body). One can produce quadruple designs by adding a forward translation[1] to two inclinations and a rotation.

Mobile statuary: Decroux named the art of moving the body *mobile statuary* (remember Decroux's vision of his father as a "moving statue"), as if the body were a Greek statue, inside a sphere, like a snowman inside a glass globe. Many types of segmented movements come under this heading and could as well be listed under the previous heading, *scales*. Undulations, compensations (parts of the body moving in opposite directions simultaneously), reestablishments (one inclined element and one vertical element reestablishing on the oblique), and all their related categories constitute mobile statuary. See Plate 4.1.

Figures of style: These include brief studies such as "The Prayer," "Salute to the Dawn," "O, Walt Whitman," and others. Figures – extended in time and space as "The Shepherd Picks a Flower for the Princess" or "The Princess Accepts the Flower" – combine elements from class work (triple designs, walks, articulations) into longer "combinations" as a ballet class will progress from *pliés* and *tendus* to combinations performed mostly in place (*adagio*) or across the floor (*enchaînements*).

Walks: Decroux spent his life in search of the ideal walk. He thought one revealed one's true self unconsciously in daily activities – in handwriting, in walking, and in the manipulation of objects. Hence, his constructed, artificial and artistic handwriting (often produced with a quill pen dipped into India ink) and his way of walking or of opening the door, all reflected his desire to achieve an artificial construction. Decroux's repertoire included one hundred walks, variations on ten basic ones. "The walk of the Poet," an inversion of the Nazi goose-steps, which he witnessed during the German occupation of Paris, obsessed him. He remarked the Nazis' forcefully extended arms and legs, leaving the trunk behind, while advocating the opposite: risking the trunk forward, arms and legs remaining behind. Thus the Poet fearlessly exposed his trunk, home to delicate and sensitive organs, to attack. The Poet, he said, believed in the goodness of human nature while the Nazi feared it.

Counterweights: This important area of Decroux's work comes directly from Hébert gymnastics. Decroux (like Lecoq [see Murray 2003: 85]) reduced acting to pushing and pulling. Counterweights and walks overlap, as walking entails counterweight, Decroux said. In order to survive, man, constructed to move vertically (bending and straightening his legs), must convert this vertical movement to the horizontal plane, resulting in the first counterweight: a reestablishment of two elements[2] on the diagonal, propelling the body into a fall. This displacement or fall, repeated, becomes a walk, and the first element of production becomes displacement.

Decroux often spoke of the importance of counterweights in the world prior to the invention of the steam engine and the internal combustion engine. In this world (all of history prior to the mid-1800s), people were dependant upon themselves and domesticated animals to accomplish all work; wind and water power (harnessed by mills and sails) provided the only exception.

Improvisation: In his last decades, in addition to daily classes, Decroux lectured Friday evenings on a wide variety of topics. Student improvisations followed these lectures. During my years there, part of my thought constantly anticipated the terrifyingly mysterious Friday night improvisations.

The first year or two, I couldn't fathom what Decroux required during these stressful and intimidating experiences. He asked individuals or small groups to stand at one end of the basement studio in a pool of what called, with a flourish of his fat fingers and mocking vocal affectation, "artistic lighting." He admonished: "Portray a thinker. After a while, you will become Thought. Emotion leads to motion, Thought begets immobility. Begin!" These enigmatic guidelines intensified rather than dispelled uneasiness surrounding the conundrum of movement/immobility, making us think that, in these improvisations, we were damned if we moved and damned if we did not.

After many years, tears, and discouragement, most eventually understood that state of being relaxed, yet alert, poised on the razor's edge, separating movement from immobility. Until then, neither our movements nor immobilities partook enough of their opposite qualities. Decroux's worst criticism, delivered in heavily accented English, was: "Human, too much human." When students had not sufficiently "evicted the tenants from the apartment," we knew it, and "God could not come to live there." These startling words from the avowed atheist meant one had to silence voices habitually filling thought with self-conscious concerns; only after completing this process of emptying out, would the moment of being "struck with a thought" become possible. Being taken over by an exterior force, yet still lucidly aware and alert, actors achieved vibrant immobility, usually followed by movement imbued with that immobility. Here, Decroux fondly quoted Chaplin: "Mime is immobility transported." After being struck with a thought, one became a thinker, working in the area of his technique known as Man in the Drawing Room (triple designs of head and bust; mostly upright torso). Further into the improvisation, with enough experience, one became what Decroux called "pure Thought," working in the domain of Mobile Statuary, using all levels of the space including the floor.

For these improvisations, Decroux insisted upon inexpressive, mask-like, noble, and beatific faces. The present-yet-absent state which accompanied such a face seemed difficult or impossible to achieve, and mysterious. But one knew who had succeeded and who had not. The first looked larger than life, radiant, almost possessed, while the latter looked uncomfortable, small, and petty. Those who succeeded looked as if they had attained a different world, whereas the others, by trying too hard, remained in this one.

WHAT DECROUX ACCOMPLISHED

Through relative success and obscurity, Decroux remained militant. He died in 1991 in the brick house his father built; students from over the world flocked there in his last decades. Its basement represented many things for Decroux, who joked "Never forget! The first Christians worshipped in catacombs!" – it was "underground" literally and metaphorically. The digging of Simplon's Tunnel (a metaphor Decroux appropriated) took years and cost lives, but finally connected France with Italy, under the Alps. Decroux dug toward "a new day" and slowly undermined established ways of doing things. He knew precious things require persistence: the militant works slowly, underground, biding his time.

Decroux's name conjures many varied images. A central figure in modern mime, everyone in the field has heard of him and many studied briefly with him. But because of his unusual perfectionism and aversion to performing, few, even among specialists, ever saw his performances. For the general public, mime was the highly visible and perennially popular Marcel Marceau; Etienne Decroux had no public recognition.

Decroux's obscurity perpetuated itself. In the 1980s, a chapter on Etienne Decroux appeared in a book on modern mime. The author admitted to having never seen anything created or performed by Decroux, live or on film, and to having never taken a lesson with Decroux, or interviewed him. With difficulty, I convinced this person to see teaching and performances of those trained by Decroux. What scholar could write a chapter on a poet whose works he had not read, or on a painter whose paintings he had not seen, even in reproduction? Due to the efforts of Eugenio Barba and ISTA (International School of Theatre Anthropology), however, scholars have begun writing about Decroux. In the series on Performance Practitioners, Decroux appears for the first time in the company of his contemporaries – Stanislavsky, Copeau, Meyerhold, and other major twentieth-century theatre reformers.

Decroux's work developed and changed over years. One era included pantomime peripherally; Marcel Marceau was a brilliant student from that period. For a time Decroux's only renown was as a teacher of Marceau and Barrault; consequently some describe Decroux as a pantomime even though he worked only briefly, and never exclusively, in this style.

Decroux's work, like Picasso's, comprises numerous styles and approaches. Like Picasso, Decroux found cubism one of several particularly fertile approaches. With Picasso the stylistic differences become apparent when paintings hang side by side; we cannot as easily evaluate Decroux's ephemeral compositions, seen by small audiences and then erased.

As one reads scrapbooks of press clippings in the Fonds Decroux in the Bibliothèque Nationale in Paris, one frequently encounters phrases, such as "magnificent ardour" describing Decroux's approach. Writers call him a "zealot of mime" and "a curious man, with fixed and fevered eyes . . . a high priest." They saw Decroux's actors as a "priestess of a mysterious cult" and "young Egyptian gods, participating in the rites of this strange religion." An especially vivid article concludes: "Etienne Decroux, who resembles a prehistoric man, plays his body as one plays a violin."

Eric Bentley's article from 1950, "The Purism of Etienne Decroux," continues in this vein:

Decroux – his baleful eyes set in his tragic mask of a face, his magniloquent language pouring out in his sinuous, wistful voice – is above all a person and a presence. A presence, one might say, and an absence. He is courteous and warm, and to that extent present, but his eyes betoken distance and an ulterior purpose. The tone of voice is gentle, but there is steel behind the velvet, an insistence, a certitude, a sense of mission. In this presence one has no doubt that all that occurs is important.

(Bentley 1953: 186–7)

Bentley describes *Ancient Combat* as the

expression of a personal vision. Although one can admire every leaf and bough, the supreme fact is that the bush burns. The work breathes a fanatic spirit. The reverberations quiver and repeat; then comes the shock, rude, shattering – but it is the old religious fanaticism, which can bide its time before it springs.

(Bentley 1953: 188)

In describing *Little Soldiers* he describes the "humorless wit, the dark fantasy, and unearthly, tremulous joy of Decroux."

Bentley finishes his essay by writing that

[e]ven if his work does not turn out to be the principal, central theatrical work of our time, it can resemble the work of some small, strict holy order from which the whole church profits.

(Bentley 1953: 195)

French mime Pinok calls studying with him "some secret initiation" (p. 64) and his house as "a place out of time where secret ceremonies unfolded" (p. 66). Another student wrote she felt "part of a holy order" describing Decroux as "of another age . . . medieval . . . mystical . . . in which there was a belief in the transformative power of art" (Wylie 1993: 110).

These writers describe Decroux and his work with a special, highly charged, vocabulary – a language of spirituality and religion, of ritual and of shamanism used in the service of art. Deidre Sklar wrote:

> Corporeal Mime is not a secret study, yet it has never been a popular form. Decroux's "puritan revolutionary" personality discourages the merely curious, and his art seems esoteric to many. Decroux's "small, strict holy order" remains outside the mainstream because he is less concerned with entertaining spectators than with transforming students – mind and body – into his image of the Promethean actor or ideal Everyman. This ideal is achieved through mastery of the physical technique of Corporeal Mime and through assimilating its theoretical principles. Students who remain with Decroux long enough to master the system have undergone a deconstruction and reconstruction process that more closely resembles ritual initiation than theatre.
>
> (Sklar 1985: 75)

While some wrote of him as a "high priest," and descriptions of his teaching and technique often stress the mystery and ceremony that surrounded his work, in his own writing, Decroux declared his "pronounced taste for . . . public things – politics and religion," and on the same page admits "hostility toward the mysterious" (Decroux 1948: 1). Decroux might confront these contradictions by asserting that nonverbal processes, that to the uninitiated seemed strange, in fact normally and scientifically complement the work he and his students carried out.

Eugenio Barba noted that Decroux "did not merely teach the 'scientific' principles of acting, but a way to *position oneself* which from posture and movement radiated to an all-embracing ethical and spiritual stance" (Barba 1997: 8). In Decroux's own words: "One must busy one's self with mime as the first Christians did with Christianity, as the first Socialists did with Socialism. We need militants" (Decroux 2003: 73).

DECROUX AND ASIAN THEATRE

Leonard Pronko's *Theatre East and West* describes how Asian forms revitalized twentieth-century theatre, not only for Copeau and Decroux, but for many others as well. The Asian strand in Decroux's work finds its origin in a version of a Noh play, *Kantan*, performed by the students at the Ecole du Vieux Colombier, which touched Decroux deeply. Although far from an accurate reconstruction, somehow these French students, under Suzanne Bing's direction, found some quality, some essential value that marked Decroux's early aesthetic development (Pronko 1967: 92). They started with a Noh play, aspired to qualities contained in a Noh play, and, judging by descriptions of the performance, the collaborators achieved a certain spare, austere aesthetic, which incorporated charged (dynamic) immobilities (Leigh 1979: 47).

Of all the twentieth-century reformers, Decroux alone left not only a philosophy, an aesthetic, and a repertory, but a vocabulary, a specific technique of moving and being on the stage, a way of achieving presence.

Like Zeami and Grotowski, Decroux seriously worked voice and text, although he considered one lifetime insufficient to realize "vocal mime" as well as Corporeal Mime. In May of 1953, age fifty-five, Decroux wrote:

> I took my first diction lesson thirty-one years ago and the last one this morning. I took my first classical dance lesson thirty-one years ago, and the last one yesterday morning. Since I left Copeau, I have done speaking theatre as a stop-gap measure and, as for movement theatre, I have thought only of it without ever dreaming of it, and I've abandoned all else to add deed to thought.
>
> (Decroux 1953: 27)

Some consider Decroux's insistence on training, similar to that required in Asian theatre, sterilizing. He compared mime study to technical study in music or dance; musicians and dancers find freedom for expression through technique. Eugenio Barba wrote: "the actor who works within a network of codified rules has a greater liberty than he who – like the Occidental actor – is a prisoner of arbitrariness and an absence of rules." Barba goes on to compare Decroux's teachings to those of Asian techniques.

> [I]n the same way that a Kabuki actor can ignore the best "secrets" of Noh, it is symptomatic that Etienne Decroux, perhaps the only European master to have elaborated a system of rules comparable to that of an Oriental tradition, seeks to transmit to his students the same rigorous closedness to theatre forms different from his own.
>
> (Barba and Savarese 1991: 8)

Correspondingly, American director and teacher Anne Bogart writes:

> To allow for emotional freedom, you pay attention to form. If you embrace the notion of containers or *katas*, then your task is to set a fire, a human fire, inside these containers and start to burn.
>
> (Bogart 2001: 103)

Decroux's compositions resemble *kata*, containing fire. The uninitiated think technique turns performers into sterile robots; the opposite is true for Decroux, Barba, and Bogart.

DECROUX AND GROTOWSKI

Some corollaries between the work of Polish theatre director Jerzy Grotowski (1933–99) and Decroux present themselves, making aspects of Decroux's work clearer. In late 1968, I stood in line in the rain for what seemed like hours, in a remote Parisian suburb, before gaining admittance to *Akropolis*, the work of a then little-known Polish director. In 1976 I saw a performance of *Apocolypsis cum Figuris*, late at night, in an unmarked building in a small unlighted street in Wroclaw, Poland, still behind the Iron Curtain. Not until Eugenio Barba's ISTA (International School of Theatre Anthropology) Tenth Meeting in Copenhagen (May 1996) did I hear Grotowski speak; certain expressions, identical word for word, like "the actor must be as relaxed as an old peasant," and others which had strong echoes, like "the only spectator is God," reminded me of Decroux. Although the style was different – Decroux's oracular thunderings contrasting Grotowski's gently diffused meanderings – something about Grotowski's uncompromising presence recalled Decroux. Later in the summer of 1996, in Pontedera, Italy, I witnessed Grotowski's collaboration with his long-time American disciple Thomas Richards. Although different in its outer manifestations, something in the intensity, the commitment, the crystal-clear quality of the work, echoed Decroux.

DECROUX, GROTOWSKI, AND THE AUDIENCE

Not just Grotowski's words, but the nature of the performance he created, recalled Decroux. Each spectator was selected, initiated, before witnessing the event, unlike public performances open to anyone with a ticket. For the three encounters listed above, Grotowski limited the audience's size – the smallest, at Pontedera, numbered only nine. In each circumstance, I had been informed especially, or personally invited to attend.

At Decroux's home in Paris, one entered first through the kitchen, and went to a simple basement studio, both workroom and "theatre." Decroux invited a limited number of initiated spectators (students in his school, a trusted neighbor, old friends), on rare occasions, for poetry readings he gave of Victor Hugo and Baudelaire or for a performance by his students. Decroux briefed the few spectators beforehand, giving them clues of what to look for. If they did not belong to his immediate circle, with his earnest arguments he tried to "convert" them before the performance.

At Pontedera, a comparable formula held. First, in a small, scrubbed kitchen (similar to Decroux's in its monastic simplicity) a senior student-actor told us (an already pre-screened group of academics and others sympathetic to the work) the rules: no foot tapping, singing, laughing, clapping, or other overt participation. He then let us read the texts used in the presentation from sheets of paper that he reclaimed before we left the kitchen. His most important admonition, however, was not, under any circumstances, to look for a plot or try to "understand." (This frame of mind, Grotowski said in his Copenhagen ISTA lectures in 1996, would only make us a blocked and unresponsive audience.) From there we went to the adjoining workroom where the event unfolded.

From the evidence, one could say that Decroux and Grotowski lost interest in the spectator as their work progressed. However, for both Decroux and Grotowski, as their careers progressed, the spectators became more and more important even as their numbers diminished. Early on, both performed (or made performances) for selected audiences, but not always small ones. As Decroux and Grotowski aged, each became more careful, valuing the experience more, treating it more carefully, and preparing the spectator (had the audience ever been given lessons in etiquette prior to a performance before?) and the actor (through years of intensive study and rehearsal) more thoroughly. Finally, for each, the only place where they could present a performance fully and without compromise became the workroom, where each closely controlled conditions. At one point Decroux usually performed for not more than ten people at a time in his dining room. He thought that in groups larger than ten, people lost their individual free will, and were incapable of seeing. After his return from New York to Paris in the early 1960s, Decroux usually chose not to perform outside his basement workroom. There were two exceptions during my time with him (1968–72). In 1970, we gave a lecture demonstration at the Maison des Jeunes et de la Culture in Rennes, and in 1971, we did two or three work demonstrations in Copenhagen. Before the presentation in Rennes, where I performed *The Carpenter* and he demonstrated arm and hand movements, our only "warm-up" occurred when he walked me back and forth across the stage behind the closed curtain. As we strolled arm in arm he told me not to worry, that everyone in the audience (as they had not yet been "converted") was an imbecile and incapable of understanding what they were about to see.

Once he said "Experimental theatre! If they want to try a *real* experiment, let them get rid of the audience!" Decroux went to great lengths, as did Grotowski, to diminish the audience's authority; it was the work that should impress. While Decroux may have never gotten rid of the audience completely, he reduced their number and their influence on the event, while maximizing the potential effect of the performance on each spectator (or *witness*, Grotowski's preferred terminology).

Grotowski told the story of an old Peking Opera actor who performed better than his young son because the former was not so eager to please the audience. He also spoke of a Russian actor whose work took on a greater depth when he learned he could easily die as a result of his onstage exertions. Grotowski said of this performer that he began acting for a different reason than to please the audience. Decroux considered pleasing the audience a kind of prostitution of the sacred art of drama. We keep coming back to Grotowski's statement: The only spectator is God.

Decroux's best words on the topic of the audience follow:

> [L]et's continue to do what we like, what we understand, and if that does not succeed for a while, don't change anything. The more we change to please the public, the less they will understand…. We must think of people's respect; to be respected, one must not lower oneself to the audience. We must wait for them to come up to us.
>
> (Decroux 2001: 33)

GROTOWSKI'S VIEW OF DECROUX'S WORK

In 1997 the College de France created the Chair of Theatre Anthropology for Grotowski. In lectures given in this capacity in Paris, Grotowski said that he had seen Decroux's work. It must have impressed Grotowski significantly because, in these lectures, he spoke of it on numerous occasions. In his inaugural lecture at Peter Brook's Bouffes du Nord, for example, he said of Decroux, that he looked for "laws of life which flow, and which finally, in an advanced phase of the work, became organized, structured, and perceptible by another." He compared this to things in nature which are expressive, but which don't try to be: the movement of the ocean, or a tree, for example. He contrasted Decroux's method with a more theatrical way of working, which had the audience in mind from the start (Grotowski 1997a). In a 1946 newspaper interview Decroux describes his way of working first for himself and not the audience:

> Beauty is like happiness, one must find it by the by, without looking for it. I make mime pieces first for my own pleasure. I learn afterwards that they also interest my friends, some workers, my concierge and the fireman on duty.
>
> (Decroux 2001: 57)

In a later lecture, Grotowski said that even though Decroux's body was aged and infirm when he saw it, Decroux radiated an inner power, something we might call spiritual strength. He saw an "illuminated purity in a ruined body" (Grotowsk 1997b).

THE VIBRATO AND DYNAMIC IMMOBILITY IN DECROUX'S WORK

In a later lecture, Grotowski used the example of Decroux to show that a performer could reach a high level of what Grotowski called "inner work" without following the same path that he himself had. Grotowski long advocated singing traditional songs which function effectively because of their "vibratory quality," influencing the singers as well as their audience. Grotowski could not have known how important vibratory quality was to Decroux, whose favorite musical instrument was the violin. When he demonstrated an exercise, Decroux played his muscles like a violin, every movement originating from a sustained vibrato in the deepest parts of the body.

There are three stories Decroux liked to tell to illustrate this quiet vibratory quality.

Story Number 1: Look at our teacher the cat! How he waits for the mouse: the body completely still, yet inside an almost imperceptible quivering, a high-pitched vibration, comes from moving yet not moving, wanting to go forward yet holding back. Then, suddenly, at the right moment, a movement of stunning efficiency and clarity: the paw extends and claws ensnare the mouse.

Story Number 2: The woman has purchased expensive cloth. Meticulously, she has pinned the pattern to it, and after careful reflection and repeated verification, she lifts the scissors, opens them, and waits. At this point of no return – before cutting – the silence is icy hot.

Story Number 3: The attentive soccer goalkeeper watches in all directions, alert, vigilant. Not wanting to do something, he wants to prevent something being done. Relaxed yet concentrated, weight equally distributed on two expectantly bent knees, ready to respond, he exemplifies the biblical citation "No one knows when the thief will come."

In *Words on Mime*, Decroux calls this quality

> mobile immobility, the pressure of water on the dike, the hovering of a fly stopped by the window pane, the delayed fall of the leaning tower which remains standing. Then similar to the way we stretch a bow before taking aim, man implodes yet again.
>
> (Decroux 1985: 51)

Decroux, almost never silent, spoke and sang constantly; he whistled, hummed, breathed loudly and buzzed as he demonstrated movements. Perhaps Grotowski did not know that Decroux taught by singing, that one of his "jokes" had him teaching singing (*enchanter*, he reminded us, meant "singing within"), while the singing school down the street taught mime (Fogal 1993: 31).

Deidre Sklar wrote that she is

> a person attuned to dynamo-rhythm [dynamic quality], which is the way the universe expresses and experiences itself. In my mind, I "sing" a reverberation of people's movement expressions with the "tocs" and vibratos I learned to think with in Decroux's basement, and, though I sometimes protest it, the *maître* stands behind me, humming in my ear.
>
> (Sklar and Cohen-Cruz 1993: 78)

Internalized singing (muscular respiration), lies at the heart of Decroux's work. A sometimes subtle, almost invisible, alternating of tense and relaxed muscles in quick succession informs Corporeal Mime. This vibration of muscles evokes the Promethean struggle that Decroux saw as the innately dramatic human condition, illustrated by three stories above, and by one below.

Whereas Decroux used vibratory quality, he also mastered dynamic immobility, using the vibratory quality, in an almost imperceptible way, while remaining (apparently) completely still. Gina Lalli describes Decroux's performance at midnight on February 3, 1958 at the Morosco Theatre in New York City (Plate 1.3):

> He talked about the principles of mime for about ten minutes. As the time passed, the audience sensed something extraordinary was happening or, perhaps, was not happening. Decroux was standing completely still, looking straight ahead. There was no gesture, no shifting of weight; only

Plate 1.3 Etienne Decroux ca. 1959 breaks a long moment of dynamic immobility in his midnight lecture demonstration at the Morosco Theatre in New York City. Unattributed photograph from the New York Public Library at Lincoln Center, Performing Arts Research Center

his lips were moving.... The audience was also compelled to be still and hardly breathed. At the end of this lecture, Decroux's left hand shot out and he swooped the heavy microphone stand overhead, in a triumphal gesture, and carried it offstage. The dramatic effect was not lost on the audience. In one gesture he had won them over. They had seen the power of the corporeal mime.

(Lalli 1993: 41)

Many of us experienced something similar, when, suddenly in the classroom the atmosphere became charged as Decroux demonstrated a simple movement with clarity and inner life, movement punctuated with immobilities exhibiting what one could call spiritual strength. Decroux said we spend a lifetime studying movement in order to remain immobile and keep the audience's interest. He often spoke of the importance of absence in presence, presence in absence.

TRANSMISSION: PATIENCE IS A LONG PASSION

Decroux said: "Now we are working on plumbing: pipes and rivets – not very exciting. But someday you will have hot steam running through those pipes." This and other stories pointed students toward a long process. "All great art is anonymous," he said. "Who is the architect of Chartres Cathedral? It will take centuries and many workers to build the Cathedral of Corporeal Mime." He attracted idealistic people to his work using charm, wit, and eloquence to "convert" them to this "Great Project," building this Cathedral of Corporeal Mime.

He suspected that he could not complete the Cathedral in his own lifetime. Without transmission through his students, his life work remains unfulfilled and he an idiosyncratic footnote in twentieth-century theatre history. An outrageous eccentric, an anomaly in twentieth-century theatre *and* the founder of an important and enduring theatre form, Decroux provided theatre practitioners and theoreticians a new way of thinking about, and doing, theatre.

Decroux challenged the predominance of playwrights and text in theatre, a paradigm that had prevailed since Aristotle, to place the actor centrally in the art. Decroux, like Grotowski, challenged the definition of the actor as someone who says the author's words and makes appropriate gestures.

TRANSMISSION OF WHAT?

Decroux constantly reinvented and rediscovered himself through his work, which constantly changed according to students' abilities or lack of them. The Decroux that Barrault and Marceau knew differed from the later Decroux and his work. What one saw in the 1950s (the time of Willi Spoor and Frits Vogels) differed from what another experienced in the early 1960s (the time of Jewel Walker and Sterling Jensen); what one witnessed in the late 1960s (Yves Lebreton and Ingemar Lindh) varied from what another lived in the 1970s (Jean Asslin, Denise Boulanger, George Molnar) or in the 1980s (Steven Wasson and Corinne Soum). Decroux fondly said: "Memory is the first artist" – memory which selects, arranges, highlights, obscures, filters. Each student has a different memory depending on his nature; depending on experiences with Decroux; and depending on who the student has since become. What one remembers today, through that artistic process of selecting, arranging, highlighting, obscuring, and filtering differs from what another remembers, and also differs from what he might have thought he saw of Decroux or of his work when he first knew him. Students' variability amplified Decroux's own.

Might we identify him as the purist who spent sixty years developing esoteric forms? The large man who dressed in stylish women's clothes and an expensive wig to perform, at Leftist political meetings in the mid-1930s, in a parody of a philanthropic member of the *haute bourgeoisie*? A man who, in the early 1920s, gave shelter to revolutionary Russian anarchist Nestor Makhno (Benhaïm 2003: 90)? Decroux and his work resemble a paperweight he valued – a faceted, crystal sphere. He loved facets in movement, and his life and work had more than that paperweight, more than one could know. Which Decroux should we remember? By preserving and transmitting all the memories of all the facets of all the work of all the Decrouxs in all the periods, we will establish the foundations of The Cathedral of Corporeal Mime, which will take centuries more to realize.

"IF CORPOREAL MIME SURVIVES, THE WORLD WILL SURVIVE"

In 1972, Decroux wrote a dedication for me in his *Paroles sur le mime*:

> One does not modernize a monument in order to conserve it. One must therefore conserve the body, which was strong, skillful, ascetic. What will

conserve it? Sport is not one of the fine arts. One gives oneself to it only to vanquish others. Dance is not a portrait of struggle. Old-fashioned pantomime is not an art of the body. Corporeal mime is more than a diversion. If it survives, the world will survive.

(Decroux 1972)

Grotowski's Paris lectures illuminate this passage: he showed a documentary from the 1950s, filmed in southern Italy, of women bitten by a tarantula, dancing the tarantella as a cure. They moved, and the musicians played and sang, not to impress spectators but to save themselves and others from death. Their expert dancing and playing, Grotowski insisted, evoked a cure. The music's strongly vibratory qualities (tambourine and violin) supported the women's shaking and trembling. Speaking of the tarantella, seemingly unrelated to Decroux's corporeal mime, Grotowski conjectured that Decroux could go beyond himself, could move for God, because of his competence and aspiration toward something surpassing spectacle. Perhaps Decroux implied this in the inscription, "corporeal mime is more than a diversion."

In writing, "If [Corporeal Mime] survives, the world will survive," did Decroux consider work in his basement a tarantella to save the world? Did Decroux imagine Corporeal Mime a cure for a world bitten by laziness, apathy, and passivity induced by mass media and increasing mechanization? Perhaps: he said that one day people would have to attend mime performances to see people working, since machines would have supplanted human physical endeavor.

Neither Decroux nor Grotowski considered theatre a "diversion." But Grotowski wondered in his tarantella lecture if Decroux consciously developed spiritual aspects of his work. Many of us know Decroux as the atheist or agnostic who nonetheless created figures entitled "God Fishes Man" and "The Prayer." He often spoke using religious metaphors, and quoted the Bible with regularity; he sang "He rests in the arms of God" while performing arm exercises based on vibrations of the biceps. I consider Decroux a spiritual person without being a religious one. (Remember his command to "empty out the apartment so that God could come to live there.") With these metaphors he admonished students to suppress nagging voices, doubts, fears, and preoccupations – mental clutter – preventing effective performance. He chose a vocabulary which mentions not only getting rid of negative influences, but welcoming positive ones. His inscription for me in a birthday copy of Bergson's *On Laughter* reads: "Paris was far. God guided you" (Decroux 1971).

Without direct reference to traditional Indian chakras, or energy centers used in Indian meditation, medicine, and theatre, Decroux made similar poetic references: a sunburst between the shoulders, the sap rising in the body as in a tree, and the fire in the stomach. Like Grotowski, Decroux acted "as if" the chakras existed. If energy rose along the spine, as Grotowski suggested when he said one must awaken the sleeping serpents at the base of the spine, Decroux started every class with such an exercise – one in which the spine itself became an awakened serpent. In Decroux's work, this "aroused" spine had to accompany an "expressionless" face which resembled those in deep meditation on statues from the Temple at Angkor.

THE GREAT PROJECT

Decroux wrote in *Words on Mime*; "I shall die a young man in the first stage of the Great Project" (Decroux 1985: 108). Does his Great Project exist, or does it exist only as a figment of Decroux's monomaniacal imagination? One of my students reported that Decroux, when his school closed definitively, seemed disoriented, shook his head and murmured "I have found nothing, I have discovered nothing." What did he find? What did he discover?

For Decroux, the Great Project, Corporeal Mime, hovered between diction and classical ballet (Decroux 1953: 27). While not necessarily silent, the silent phase of reconquering the body and reestablishing the actor's centrality in the theatre had to precede the reintroduction of the voice and text. Like Zeami and Grotowski, Decroux based his theories firmly on the physical practice of theatre rather than on literature.

At the first stage of his Great Project, Decroux ingrained principles into students' bodies and minds. He wanted them to continue working on this Cathedral of Corporeal Mime, a project requiring workers over generations. His work, requiring self-sacrifice and a long-term commitment, contradicted twentieth-century visions of instant wealth and glory. His teaching, as political as it was artistic, engaged the whole person, not the performer alone.

Often his teaching – or ingraining – process, used vibrations, audible and silent, created by singing or by moving muscles in alternating currents of tension and relaxation. Often he placed parts of students' bodies where they should go, with an urgent insistence and vibratory quality. Often, like the teacher of Noh drama, he pulled back against an arm or a leg to show how much resistance one had to offer to movement. He pronounced the word "resistance" with an especially incisive diction, allowing no misunderstanding.

Can Decroux's teaching continue if it assimilates into mainstream theatre? Does Corporeal Mime exist as a separate entity, or only as one more "movement-for-actors" tool? Decroux, haunted by these questions, treated them in many Friday night lectures. While theatre influenced by Decroux might exist, aside from these artistic accidents, what about daily teaching to serious students over a long period, and the continued teaching and performance of his repertoire? Now we must carefully watch the second generation, students of Decroux's students, to see how the Great Project progresses.

Others will judge whether Decroux's technique has aspects of inner work comparable to the Noh actor's or Grotowski's. History will determine whether to make of him a twentieth-century Zeami: founder of a new theatre whose repertoire will continue for centuries, and whose different schools pass down a slightly different repertoire or slightly different versions of the same repertoire. On the other hand, perhaps Decroux's technique will become assimilated into the hundreds of other "movement-for-actors" possibilities. Construction on the Cathedral might continue while, elsewhere, its framework supports and is covered over by other vastly different architectural designs.

NOTES

1 One can easily imagine inclining or rotating the head, or some other part of the body. A translation, however, one imagines less easily, as it requires the part of the body under the translated part to incline: for example, the neck will incline to the right as the head remains vertical and translates to the right. (See Figure 4.11).

2 This technical term refers to one element (part of the body) inclined to one direction, the top element resting on an imaginary inclined line. When the lower vertical element moves toward the diagonal line, the upper element joins it, reestablishing on to the oblique, which the upper element had previously touched.

SUMMARY AND ANALYSIS
OF *WORDS ON MIME*[1]

Etienne Decroux's *Paroles sur le Mime*, first published in France in 1963, appeared in English as *Words on Mime* in 1985 and subsequently in Japanese, Spanish, and Italian. The first mime to have written a book on his art, Decroux inadvertently gives us an intellectual, passionate, artistic, argumentative, polemical, and poetic self-portrait – through its pages we see him laboriously carving a new art form, Corporeal Mime, from the quarry of his imagination and from his own and his students' resistant flesh.

Near the end of this collection of articles, gleaned from over thirty years of notes, manifestos, projects, and evaluations written in a lapidary and sometimes impenetrable style, Decroux articulates his book's theme and fundamental observation: "Western theatre is not an art" (p. 149).

European theatre mostly used its all-too-quotidian actors' bodies to "suggest the thing by the thing itself" (p. 29) – for example, old men performing the roles of old men, young women performing the roles of young women, etc. – and thereby disqualified itself as art by Decroux's definition: "For an art to be, the idea of one thing must be given by another thing" (p. 30). Corporeal Mime defamiliarized the actor's body, demanding physical artifice and articulation, and revealed the actor's potential as a vehicle for art.

In teaching, Decroux held up two imaginary roses, one plastic, the other real, asking the class, "Which embodies the artistic?" The student who guessed the plastic, articulated, and artificial rose guessed correctly.

Man could take no credit for the real rose, Decroux said, more beautiful but made by God. Decroux's exasperation at this basic confusion explains his disdain for traditional Western theatre, which he saw as the logical extension of the

> sideshow exhibiting the bearded woman, the giant and the dwarf, the hydrocephalic child and the two bodies linked by a single head, a foreshadowing of orthodox theatre or of its perfected form: the cinema.
>
> (p. 29)

Although Decroux earned his living from this orthodox theatre and cinema, he worked with a revolutionary zeal to make the human body artificial, artistic, by transforming it into a keyboard, whose divisions were: head, hammer (a combination of head and neck), bust (head, neck, and chest), torso (head, neck, chest, and waist), trunk (head, neck, chest, waist, and pelvis), demi-Eiffel (from head to knees), and Eiffel Tower (the whole body). He viewed the body in the same way as would a "craftsman making a string marionette, or a sculptor making an articulated model" (p. 70). This primary premise differs astonishingly from anything proposed in Western theatre heretofore, except by Edward Gordon Craig and his *ubermarionette*. But Decroux, unlike Craig, found a way to make his vision of an articulated actor a reality (see Plate 2.1).

Western acting of whatever school (with the possible exception of Commedia dell'arte) had not, until Decroux, articulated the actor's body to the same degree as Western dance. Decroux's work articulated the actor's body in a detailed and complex way, surpassing in number, nature, and complexity the articulations of Western dance.

Below, I follow the chapter headings from *Words on Mime* as we examine Decroux's world-view – his life-long, Promethean attempt to make Western theatre an art in his definition of the word, rather than what he saw primarily as a display of idiosyncratic personality.

CHAPTER 1: SOURCES

DECROUX "DISCOVERS" CORPOREAL MIME, OR IT IS "REVEALED" TO HIM

In Chapter 1 of *Words on Mime*, Decroux acknowledges two primary sources of Corporeal Mime: his first teacher, French stage director and

Plate 2.1 Etienne Decroux ca. 1959 improvises with a cane in his midnight lecture demonstration at the Morosco Theatre in New York City. Unattributed photograph from the New York Public Library at Lincoln Center, Performing Arts Research Center

teacher Jacques Copeau, and British theoretician Edward Gordon Craig. In the following discussion we will see how important Copeau was to Decroux's project, why Decroux often claimed to have invented only his own belief in Corporeal Mime – that while he had raised the child, Copeau was the true father of Corporeal Mime (Decroux 1942: 6).

JACQUES COPEAU

When Decroux auditioned for Copeau, October 15, 1923, Copeau noted the twenty-five-year-old's good voice and correct speech, and praised his simplicity (Copeau 2000: 273). Admitted for the 1923–24 school year, Decroux stood out because of the "cut of his suit, hat, large bow-tie of the early militant socialists . . . and his verbosity awed his fellow students, who nicknamed him 'the orator.'" Already a purist, he often repeated "Above art there is politics, above art there is politics . . . . Art is a publicity seeker, truth a saint; a saint should never lower herself, no matter how ugly she may be, before a publicity seeker" (Dorcy 1975: 42–3).

Able, yet inexperienced, Decroux immediately plunged into Copeau's world: the rarified atmosphere of Paris' intellectual and artistic elite, populated by the likes of novelist André Gide, and actors Charles Dullin and Louis Jouvet, among many brilliant others. Copeau, an idealist-visionary who used the theatre as a laboratory to verify long-held artistic hypotheses, strongly impressed Decroux, who observed his teacher's passionate dedication to the renewal of theatre in all its aspects, and admired his "appetite for the absolute" (p. 3). Reacting against the glitz of commercial theatre, the stodginess of the Comédie Française, and the naturalism of André Antoine, Copeau proposed instead a respect for classic texts (both French and in translation); fixed stage architecture, and the rejection of painted scenery; poetic stylization in staging; expressive yet not showy ensemble acting; and performance for an elite, cultivated, and honest public. In short, Copeau advocated a "low overhead, naked theatre" (Copeau 2000: 151). Copeau's insatiable "appetite for the absolute" soon became Decroux's own and, during his career, Decroux took Copeau's "naked theatre" to degrees undreamed of by his mentor.

Copeau intuited the intimate relationship between acting style and theatre architecture. For example, melodrama actors, like white-faced pantomimes, performed for best visibility with faces and hands thrust forward into the footlights, their backs correspondingly curved; called "crabs" because of their sideways manner of walking, melodrama actors never turned away from the footlights. In his theatre on the rue du Vieux-Colombier, Copeau covered the orchestra pit to bring the stage out into the audience. He abolished footlights and placed lighting sources above the actors, enabling them to straighten their spines and stand perpendicular to the earth as their forbears had done in what Copeau called the Golden Ages of drama – the Greek, Commedia dell'arte, Noh, and Elizabethan theatres. In these Golden Ages, performances were often held outdoors in natural light, and the use of masks was common. Copeau considered the circus ring an important example:

> Clowns are not pedants like actors; they are sincere, naive. They perform a difficult and modest craft. They are the distant descendants of the old Italian Commedia actors who did not turn up their noses at mixing physical *tours de force* and extraordinary suppleness into their brilliant acting.
>
> (Copeau 2000: 178)

Accordingly, Copeau's teaching staff at the Vieux-Colombier School included Parisian intellectuals as well as circus clowns, poets, actors, dancers, and sculptors. Decroux entered this artistic hothouse, and began to grow and cross-pollinate there.

Someone had to actively hold together a school whose curriculum comprised such disparate disciplines. This task fell not to Copeau, the dreamer and visionary consumed by the grueling work of raising money to keep his theatre afloat, but to Suzanne Bing, a leading actress in the company, without whom "the school would have remained nothing more than a project, or ended up like the others: chaos" (p. 1). Copeau's daughter, Marie-Hélèn (later Dasté), who "[j]oin[ed] in our pranks with a knowing smile," constituted the third member of what Decroux describes as a "happy trinity" (p. 3) that prevented life at the school from becoming morose.

Decroux itemizes the classes students took at the Ecole du Vieux-Colombier. Though they may seem not so unlike the classes actors study today, in 1920, Copeau's pedagogy departed radically from that of every other school in the world. Copeau proposed

> ground acrobatics, stadium athletics, ordinary gymnastics, classical ballet, corporeal mime, voice production, ordinary diction, declamation of classical chorus and of Japanese Nō, singing and sculpting. History of music,

of costume, of philosophy, of literature, of poetry, of theatre and of much more besides . . . . We were obliged to attend all the classes.

(p. 2)

Notice in the list of classes the words "corporeal mime." Twenty years later Decroux wrote: "Copeau is truly the father of mime which is called corporeal; and I raised the child" (Decroux 1942: 6). In this text, when referring to Copeau's instigation, I will use lower case – corporeal mime, but when mentioning Decroux's life-long project, I will capitalize – Corporeal Mime.

The idea for Corporeal Mime first came to Decroux in Copeau's class, in which Copeau had his students cover their faces with veils and inexpressive masks. Copeau's desire, which became Decroux's obsession, was to thus transfer the capacity of expression from the face – a doorway to ham acting – to the almost-nude body, which became the actor's new expressive "face." Later, Decroux enumerated qualities he observed at the Ecole du Vieux-Colombier:

I had never seen slow-motion movement before. I had never seen prolonged immobilities, or explosive movements followed by sudden petrifaction. The actors all had harmonious bodies – not well-articulated bodies – but harmonious ones that were pleasant to watch.

(Decroux 1978: 39)

WHAT DECROUX LEARNED *CHEZ* COPEAU

Copeau's revolutionary approach revealed what the body said without words and without the grimaces and gestures reminiscent of nineteenth-century pantomime. Students improvised simple actions: actions used in trade, by craftsmen or by manual laborers, and imitations of animals and machines. Sometimes participants planned their improvisations, briefly, among themselves; at other times, Copeau or Bing gave a word and students expressed spontaneously what it suggested. Students performed exercises based on spring, the growth of plants, wind in trees, and sunshine. Decroux describes the exercises this way:

The manner of playing resembled the slow motion of film. But while that is the slowing down of fragments of reality, ours was the slow production of one gesture in which many others were synthesized.

> This process, already intelligible, was beautiful.
>
> We reproduced noises of the town, of the house, of nature, the cries of animals. All of this with the mouth, the hands and the feet.
>
> (p. 4)

The fertile limitations by which Copeau inspired his students' improvisations became the cornerstone for Decroux's Corporeal Mime.

In 1924, two performances touched Decroux: in March, students performed a Noh play, *Kantan*, directed by Suzanne Bing, and in June, students presented their own compositions. As a first-year auditor, Decroux could not participate in these projects.

For the March 1924 performances, Copeau and Bing identified *Kantan* as a reinterpretation of Noh, not a reconstruction – neither Copeau nor Bing had seen or studied that form. Western flute and drum substituted for Japanese instruments, and language, stage dimensions, and masks differed from the original. A lead actor's injury required cancellation of a performance scheduled for March 1924; nonetheless, students showed the play in rehearsal for Copeau, André Gide, the British playwright Harley Granville-Barker, and the students of the school.

The intensity of the actors' simple gestures moved Bing to tears. Granville-Barker, also moved, congratulated the students on how much they had accomplished in three years. Copeau considered it "one of the jewels, one of the secret riches of the work of the Vieux-Colombier" (1931: 100). Michel Saint-Denis remembered it as the "incomparable summit of our work in Copeau's School/Laboratory" (quoted in Rudlin 1986: 49). Decades later, Decroux pronounced it "the only time in my life where I felt *the art* of diction" (Kusler 1974: 151). Gide alone remained unmoved by the performance and skeptical of this specialized direction in Copeau's work.

Decroux described the June 1924 end-of-year performance, based on the improvisations the students had developed during the year, as "the most beautiful thing I have ever seen in the theatre" (Kusler 1974: 151). He described it in 1939:

> Sitting quietly among the spectators, I beheld an astonishing show.
>
> It consisted of mime and sounds. The whole performance took place without a word, without any make-up, without costumes, without a single

> lighting effect, without properties, without furniture and without
> scenery.
>
> The development of the action was skillful enough for them to condense
> several hours into a few seconds, and to contain several places in only
> one. . . .
>
> The acting was moving and comprehensible, of both plastic and musical
> beauty.
>
> (p. 5)

In this description, we see the beginnings of Decroux's poor theatre: no
text, no costumes, no make-up, no stage lighting, props, or furniture.
The sounds Decroux mentions doubtless served as the basis of his life-
long interest in Vocal Mime, an art he regretted not having time to
develop. Decroux famously used *raccourcis* throughout his career, and we
see these condensations of time and space mentioned here. Finally, he
mentions the musical (dynamically phrased) and plastic (sculptural)
quality of the movement.

These two "Japanese" performances influenced Decroux's
subsequent work so much that years later, succeeding Jacques Lecoq as
movement teacher and coach at Giorgio Strehler's Piccolo Teatro in
Milan, he told Lecoq that he hoped to make the Italians move like
Japanese actors (Lecoq 1980; personal interview).

COPEAU'S STYLE OF ACTING AND
HOW IT INFLUENCED DECROUX

Copeau encouraged a particular acting style among the actors in his
theatre and among the students in his school:

> Anyone who has not seen Boverio, Jouvet, and Copeau together in *The
> Brothers Karamazov* will never, I fear, fully understand the importance of a
> single word, the density of gesture, an ominous silence, the expressive
> force excluding every external device, in short, the significance of style.
>
> (Dorcy 1961: 8)

In hiring actors, Copeau sought, sometimes perhaps unconsciously, the
qualities he uncovered in students – the qualities that permeate Noh
theatre, and that later became essential to Decroux's Corporeal Mime:
simplicity, austerity, clarity, articulateness, and gravity.

Decroux spoke of this style, as embodied by Jouvet and Dullin, two of Copeau's most important actor-collaborators:

> There was something in Jouvet's instinct, in his temperament, that I liked. I felt in his work the beginnings of, a taste for, the marionette... a certain way of turning the head, of using his neck, a certain way of taking his place on the stage. One sensed in him the articulated man .... Dullin took me in a completely rudimentary form, he instructed me, he formed me. He showed me what it was to give my all, and he kept me from overshooting the mark. He tried to give me what is called good taste – the taste for just enough, while still having passion. How exciting it was to work with him! His acting excited me more than anyone else's. But that doesn't mean I liked it as a doctrine! From the point of view of doctrine, the idea (for mime) comes from the Ecole du Vieux-Colombier, from Copeau, and the style came to me with Jouvet.
>
> (Decroux 1978: 14)

THE IDEA OF THE SCHOOL

Copeau sought to reform the theatre, conferring upon it "a dignity and religious essence" (Copeau 2000: 205). To do this, he had to train actors himself (Copeau 2000: 227). He valued the school not only as a prelude to performance but as a laboratory, as an end in itself. Not surprisingly, Copeau eventually sacrificed his company in favor of the school; his overwhelming passion for research (as well as his distrust of actors' *cabotinage* – ham acting) manifested in Decroux's career. Only coincidentally facilitating Decroux's acting career, more importantly, Copeau opened a path of research.

THE MASKED OR VEILED FACE

While theatre commercialism countered the religious origins of performance (still evident in many non-Western theatres), Decroux, Copeau, and others sought a "religious" rather than a "commercial" approach, and developed this taste in their followers. Nineteenth-century French actor Mounet-Sully is credited with saying, of a failed performance, "The gods did not descend." Metaphors – language describing an ideal acting state – emerge from the writings of Decroux and others who worked with Copeau: Jean Dasté, Michel St Denis,

Charles Dullin, and Jean Dorcy. All frequently use terms which today seem received terminology to describe the actor's experience; having become everyday words, they have lost, in part, their original strength. Nonetheless, they astonish us if we hear them anew: Dasté used the word "possessed," saying he experienced "moments of frenzy." Copeau describes a character who "comes from outside, takes hold of him, and replaces him." Dorcy uses the word "trance." An actor under Copeau's direction in *The Brother's Karamazov* used Dullin's vocabulary – "altered state of consciousness" – to describe how he continued to act, after having been seriously injured on stage. And Decroux said that, after "evicting the tenant" the actor should be "inhabited by God."

Decroux noted that Copeau had restored physical truth to these images by rediscovering the mask – an antidote to ham acting. While masked exercises are now commonplace, when Copeau introduced them into the mainstream of Western theatre training, he did so in the context of a Cartesian country of reason and clarity that had forgotten the mask's power. The mask, a shamanic tool, developed a kind of sincerity and presence in acting, forgotten in the West with the death of Commedia dell'arte. With only a superficial knowledge of non-Western approaches, Copeau and friends discovered intuitively a tool used in non-Western theatre and ritual, writing and speaking about it using a precise vocabulary.

The mask: shamanic tool for actor training

David Cole's paradigm seems an ideal optic for viewing the mask work Decroux learned at Copeau's school. Cole asserts in *The Theatrical Event* that one may view theatrical activity as: (1) a shamanistic quest, a psychic journey to the world of the script, followed by (2) a psychic takeover (called rounding or possession) by the script character of the actor, and subsequently (3) a return to the everyday world, where the inspired performance of the possessed actor reaches an attentive audience. While he does not claim sacred dimensions or religious functions for drama as Copeau did later in his life, Cole finds ritual practices useful analogies for theatrical ones:

> Shamanic activity and possession behavior frequently resemble theatre, while contemporary rehearsal and actor-training methods often recall the practices of shamans and possession specialists. In the moment of an

actor's passing from shamanic voyager to possessed vehicle, the theatre, as an event, is born.

(Cole 1975: v)

Jean Dorcy, in a passage reminiscent of Cole, yet written decades before, detailed how to put on the mask:

Here are the rites I followed so as to be ready to perform masked:

(a) Well seated in the middle of the chair, not leaning against the back of the seat. Legs spaced to ensure perfect balance. The feet flat on the ground.

For beginning the search, Dorcy advises the actor (shaman) to relax yet remain alert (back away from back of chair). Note his use of the word "rite."

(b) Stretch the right arm horizontally forward, shoulder high; it holds the mask, hanging by its elastic. The left hand, also stretched out, helps to shoe the mask, thumb holding the chin, index and second finger seizing the opening of the mouth.
(c) Simultaneously inhale, close the eyes, and shoe the mask.

Dorcy gives in "b" a practical yet codified way to put the mask on. In "c," the shaman/actor must block out reality by closing the eyes. Simultaneously, he puts on the tool which will transport him to a different world.

(d) Simultaneously breathe and place forearms and hands on the thighs. The arms, as well as the elbows, touch the torso, fingers not quite reaching the knees.
(e) Open the eyes, inhale, then simultaneously close the eyes, exhale and bend the head forward. While bending the head, the back becomes slightly rounded. In this phase, arms, hands, torso and head are completely relaxed.

Dorcy advises total relaxation creating the void, prior to what Decroux called "evicting the tenant." The next step shows this forceful eviction.

(f) It is here, in this position, that the clearing of the mind occurs. Repeat mentally or utter, if this helps, during the necessary time (2, 5, 10, 25 seconds), "I am not thinking of anything, I am not thinking of

> anything . . . ." If, through nervousness, or because the heart was beating
> too strongly, the "I am not thinking of anything" was ineffective,
> concentrate on the blackish, grey, steel, saffron, blue or other shade
> found inside the eye and extend it indefinitely in thought; almost
> always, this shade blots out conscious thought.

Note here the operative words: "blot out conscious thought."

> (g)   Simultaneously, inhale and sit upright, then exhale and open your eyes.
>
> Now, the masked actor, sufficiently recollected, can be inhabited by
> characters, objects, thoughts; he is able to perform dramatically.

> (Dorcy 1975: 108–9)

Copeau's remedy for sick theatre, his empty stage, required new actors to inhabit it. This empty stage finds a corollary in the actor's shamanic void. The mask became Copeau's principal tool, enabling actors to live interior and exterior silence, to walk the razor's edge of dynamic immobility. The mask permitted Copeau's actors to rejoin the Golden Ages of theatre – ancient Greek theatre, the Japanese Noh, the Commedia dell'arte. Using masks, they transformed the empty stage through presence, not primarily through literature, music, costumes, or decor.

Contemporary parallels become apparent when dancers in the Alvin Ailey company speak of "crossing over" during performance (reported to me by Anna Deavere Smith in conversation); not speaking as anthropologists, they simply describe what they do. Possibly what we describe as "shamanic" in some cultures has always existed in European performance as well. Actors, before often considered heretical because of what Copeau described as their "*commerce étrange*," certainly spoke or wrote cautiously about practices that could further alienate them from society. Between King David's dance before the Ark of the Covenant and Molière's burial in unconsecrated ground, a break in the actor/dancer's role occurred. Copeau and Decroux set about mending it.

Mask exercises at the Vieux-Colombier taught Decroux how the nude body could achieve maximum visibility and impact on Copeau's bare stage, after first having emptied itself of quotidian thought. The nude body, on a bare stage, glowed with an inner light when actors successfully "emptied out the apartment" and when "God came to live there."

Copeau's mask proved a tool for actors' altered consciousness; Decroux's body (transformed by Corporeal Mime) became that mask, created from the inside as Copeau's masks were sculpted from the outside. This circular history begins when Copeau's first mask classes, called corporeal mime, inspired Decroux to create Corporeal Mime, the form which in its turn became a heightened version of Copeau's mask. Decroux's first disciple, Jean-Louis Barrault, wrote, after his studies with Decroux, "My body has become a face" (Barrault 1972: 73), and Decroux extolled the "entire body that becomes a face" (p. 130).

Copeau emphasized training actors from childhood, before they become worldly, and of "renormalizing" adult actors. Decroux's teaching changed students' spines, articulation patterns and possibilities, breathing, and, through improvisations, encouraged them to new levels of consciousness. Decroux gave students special names and different colored ropes (used in training) when they became "initiated" – *anciens élèves* [advanced students] who performed only for "believers." For most, study with Decroux implied radical language and culture changes. And yet, many Asian theatre and martial arts consider normal what seems extraordinary in Decroux's and Copeau's teaching.

Decroux was sufficiently touched by Copeau's fervor that fifty years after their encounter – and despite their very different politics, temperament, and socioeconomic and educational level – he still remembered Copeau with affection and respect. Decroux always generously attributed to Copeau's corporeal mime class the first impulse for his own project.

EDWARD GORDON CRAIG

Craig used theoretical writing and stage designs as offensive weapons to liberate theatre from Victorian clutter and sentimentality on one hand, and from the new realism that opposed them, on the other. Craig's antinaturalistic, non-illusionistic stage design, like Copeau's bare stage, invited movement while strongly suggesting a role for theatre that surpassed the mere interpretation of literature.

In his three short essays on Craig, Decroux explains Craig's opposition to realism and its chief advocates, Stainslavsky in Russia and Antoine in France. Decroux remembers, and mentions approvingly, seven of Craig's observations on the actor. As we read them, we cannot help seeing how closely they resemble Decroux's own assertions:

1   In performance, the actor's "mind must exploit his emotion and not his emotion his mind. This state of intoxication is to be particularly discouraged in a work of artifice."
2   "[S]tyle and symbol are qualities essential to art."
3   The actor should study for six years before appearing on stage.
4   An actor should not immodestly exhibit "explosions of his inner self."
5   Actors should "seek inspiration by the methods used by other artists."
6   Actors must not allow other artists to "colonize" the theatre.
7   Actors must work to discover "laws of the theatre" and not proceed by guesswork.

(p. 6)

Decroux and Craig, however, seem not in perfect agreement on the *ubermarionette*, the ideal (or super) marionette. Could a living actor truly embody these seven points? Craig seems to have wavered in his conclusions; did he literally mean a wooden object should replace live actors, or did he argue for a live actor inspired by a wooden object, whose virtues, Decroux argues, can only be acquired by "practicing a specially applied form of gymnastics" (p. 7) – Corporeal Mime? Craig might have thought (at different times, or concurrently) either, or both.

Decroux does not keep us wondering about his conviction, however. He states unequivocally that he wishes for "the birth of this actor made of wood," a "large-scale marionette arousing, by its appearance and its movements, a feeling of seriousness and not of condescension" inspiring "terror and pity, and, from there, ris[ing] to the level of the waking dream" (p. 8). But, he cautions us, only the study of Corporeal Mime (a study that could only be made on the living human form) could prepare one for such an undertaking.

When he wonders if the "famous theatrical experiments of Russia in 1928 [would] have ever seen the light of day if Craig's ideas had not spread across Europe at the beginning of the century," is Decroux telling us that perhaps his own work would have been equally impossible without Craig? The theatre world had long considered Craig a mere dreamer, a man incapable of realizing in production his dreams or his drawings;

Decroux saw him otherwise, and concludes by defending Craig against the criticism that he "achieved nothing" and salutes him as "our leader" (p. 9).

OTHER INFLUENCES

Decroux itemizes other influences in his "Autobiography relative to the genesis of corporeal mime." His love of sculpture combines with a love of poetry to create the following prose-poem, extolling the beauty of Corporeal Mime:

> "Pensée, poussée, pouce et pincée," which in French are almost homonyms, are also almost synonymous. ("Thought, pushed, thumb, pinched.") Our thought pushes our gestures in the same way that the thumb of the sculptor pushes forms; and our body, sculpted from the inside, stretches. Our thought, between its thumb and index-finger, pinches us along the reverse flap of our envelope and our body, sculpted from the inside, folds.
>
> Mime is, at the same time, both sculptor and statue.

(p. 12)

Decroux also lists his natural attributes which contributed to the creation of Corporeal Mime: his strength, suppleness, gift for imitation, analysis, and explanation; his love of doing and demonstrating.

Decroux describes how he "discovered" Corporeal Mime, his "Revelation in Three Phases": the café-concert, Georges Carpentier, and Jacques Copeau.

Café-concert

In 1909, when he was eleven years old, Decroux's father took him to a performance in a wooden building on the banks of the river Seine. There he saw "dangerous juggling and acrobatics" of performers whose "faces expressed the state of the hero in action, without distracting us from the bodies which were performing that action" (p. 14).

> Although this act was just the skeleton of a story, with no moral and no depth of character, it was an example of corporeal mime.
>
> The actors lived their story, unconscious of being heroes, and therefore did not express it.

(p. 14)

Here too he witnessed the last gasps of nineteenth-century pantomime, which "displeased" him for the same reasons that the previous performance favorably impressed him. The Pierrot told his audience, without words, the tale of his love, his misfortune, his crime and his punishment. The speaking actor is less garrulous (p. 14).

Decroux would have us believe that he developed his distaste for conscious "expression" and his preference for "doing" and "being," at a very early age.

The boxer Georges Carpentier (1894–1975)

Known as the "orchid man" for the flower he often wore in his buttonhole, Georges Carpentier became vastly popular through his elegant bearing, agile footwork, and gentlemanly fighting style. After retiring from the ring, he succeeded as a handsome film actor. For Decroux, he marked a sea change, from the rotund diner Roger Shattuck describes in his book about Belle Epoque France, *The Banquet Years*, to the slender young student characterized by "[v]igor and grace; strength, elegance; dazzle and thought; a taste for danger and a smile" (p. 14). Carpentier reflects the age in which France rediscovered the Olympic Games, and Germany popularized *korperkulture* and nudism.

Jacques Copeau

Here Decroux tells us again that Copeau invented corporeal mime, and that all Decroux invented was his belief in it.

The comic café-concert performance exuded superficiality. As a reality, Carpentier, while a "noble model," could not become art; only Copeau's teaching revealed to him

> a performing art that represents through body movement, that could shelter under its vast roof not only that which causes laughter but also that which arouses terror, pity and the waking dream . . . . It had already been put into practice at the Vieux-Colombier school.

(p. 15)

Decroux, equally in love with Corporeal Mime and politics, gives us his explosive "Doctrinal Manifesto" at the close of this section. Here he explains that for Copeau mime functioned as a part of theatre, while

Decroux saw theatre as part of mime, as "mime is the essence of theatre, which in turn is the accident of mime" (p. 15). Decroux gets to the heart of Corporeal Mime's refusal of plot and situation, its love of movement for its own sake and not as a representation of something else, when he writes that the "only event shown here is the event itself" (p. 16).

CHAPTER 2: THEATRE AND MIME

DECROUX CREATES THE "ACTOR ART"

Decroux begins with an article dedicated to Georges Pomiès (self-taught French modern dance pioneer, 1902–33) entitled "My Definition of Theatre," which confirms his belief in "the main points, namely: that one must rehearse a play before writing it; and that the theatre is the actor art, which proves that, as an art of the beautiful, theatre does not exist" (p. 27).

Decroux defines theatre as *l'art d'acteur* or "the actor art" (an intentionally awkward juxtaposition of words – both in French and in English translation – intended to slow the reader down) because all arts must have a home. Painting, sculpture, architecture, music, literature, and dance all have a home base before mixing in the theatre; "every art enjoys the privilege of expressing the world in its own way, without calling on any other art" (p. 23). The only art which does not, and hence "does not exist" is the actor art. To remedy this situation, Decroux proposes in the theatre "[f]or a period of thirty years, the proscription of every alien art" (p. 26). For Decroux, the confounding of literature, the pernicious interloper, with theatre was an "evil so deeply rooted that it is revealed in the vocabulary: what we call 'play' is the printed text." (Decroux's remark of seventy years ago is still true in France today where the word "theatre" means printed play text.) An advocate of "poor theatre" well before Grotowski coined the phrase (Grotowski 2002), and of "postdramatic theatre" half a century before Hans-Thies Lehmann (Lehman 2006), Decroux posed the question: what can an actor do without script, costume, décor, lighting, music, and choreography? Whatever remained became "the actor art." And where "does one see the art of the actor as one sees painting: in its pure state?" Decroux had to develop Corporeal Mime to answer this question.

Decroux continues with these reasonable words:

> There is no proof that by its progress, pure theatre [Corporeal Mime] will compensate for the loss of the auxiliary arts [literature, stage design, music, dance, singing, etc.]... The undertaking does not furnish the proof. What is worse, it requires will-power and imagination. It is a matter of cutting off the theatre's right hand.

(p. 27)

Decroux certainly had the will-power and the imagination to perform the above described surgery, and in the process to make a "pure theatre" or "actor art." He observes with startling clarity that

> since the actor is the only artist without a home of his own, the theatre must become his property.
>
> Such a measure will not force him to drive out his old colonizers, but will enable him, finally free to make his open-houses less frequent.

(p. 24)

IN CREATING THE "ACTOR ART," DECROUX RE-ENVISIONED THE HUMAN BODY

In developing Corporeal Mime, Decroux constructed a new actor, akin to Craig's *ubermarionette*, by reimagining, recontextualizing, rethinking, and defamiliarizing the body. He broke the body into new units, and gave it a different way of meaning. Barthes reminds us, "our society takes the greatest pains to conjure away the coding of the narrative situation" as "bourgeiois society and the mass culture issuing from it ... demand signs which do not look like signs" (Barthes 1977: 116). Decroux's newly minted body purposely looked like a sign, a highly and visibly articulated one. Decroux wanted the sign to look like a sign so much that he said one had to perform as if slapping the audience to keep them awake.

The nineteenth-century author of *The Aesthetics of Movement*, Paul Souriau, understood this point well:

> Grace... is obtained not by giving the perfect illusion of nature, but, on the contrary, by underlining the methodical elements of the movement.
>
> The more I reflect on the theory by which art, in its various manifestations,

has to be concealed and appear absent, the less it seems to me in accord with the real requirements of taste.

(Souriau 1983: 94)

Decroux, Barthes, and Souriau saw art as articulation and artifice. Decroux reconfigured the body as follows:

The face: Corporeal Mime covers the face to reveal what the trunk (the *core* or *corpus*) can say without it. After working with an inexpressive mask or a veil, Decroux discovered they drew almost as much attention as the expressive face. He proposed instead a translucently inexpressive face, one which avoided grimacing but which instead changed like clouds moving slowly across the sky. While working at a hospital he met a demandingly cruel old man, whose difficult personality had distorted his face. The day this man died, his face changed instantly from one warped by anger and distrust into a noble sculpture. Decroux wanted that transformed face in Corporeal Mime.

The hands: Decroux distrusted the hands almost as much as he did the face since they were co-partners in the deceit of nineteenth-century pantomime. Decroux made a repertoire for hands – shell, daisy, trident, salamander, porcelain doll, designation, and others – so that the hands never found themselves in a natural position.

The arms: The arms, since they carry the hands, became guilty by association. Decroux said that since you cannot unscrew them and put them into a drawer, you must study and master them, or they become painfully obvious. One day in the late 1940s, running after someone on the street, he injured his ankle. Returning home, his foot covered in plaster, he sat dejectedly on this bed. He looked up and saw his reflection in the *armoire à glace*. Struck with the idea of adapting, for the arms, movements he had discovered for body, Decroux researched continuously for months until the ankle healed. By inventing the newly defamiliarized hands and arms, and working through conceptual problems in the trunk, he enriched his technique immeasurably.

The shoulders: "God does not have shoulders" he shouted at hapless students caught making forbidden, "expressive" shoulder movements. Associated with passion, anger, fear, and other "hot" states, Decroux's classically cool lexicon rejected them as well as their corollaries, the hips. Shoulders and hips moving together cast the body into an erotic or sensual mode Decroux considered inappropriate for the stage.

The legs and feet: Decroux called them the "proletariat" of the body. He described an ocean liner with the first-class passengers dressed in white, sitting in deck chairs, drinking champagne, while below the stevedores, covered with black dust and sweating profusely, stoked the furnaces with shovelfuls of coal. In this analogy, the head, the arms and hands represented the first-class passengers, while the workers below decks became the trunk, legs, and feet.

In the analogy of horse and rider, legs and feet became the horse, the trunk the rider. Copeau's school convinced Decroux that ballet trained the legs and feet ideally.

The trunk: For Decroux, the head, neck, chest, waist, and pelvis – the trunk – constituted the core or essence of a person: one could procreate, vote, and had to pay taxes, so long as the truck remained intact. The trunk became the basis of Decroux's art. No other technique articulates the trunk in the detail that Corporeal Mime does; no other technique requires the trunk to become, as Barrault said, a face.

THE "ACTOR ART" MOVES WITH A CERTAIN DYNAMO-RHYTHM

Dynamo-rhythm, the term Decroux coined to discuss speed and weight, reveals itself through pause, weight, resistance, hesitation, and surprise – basic elements of drama. Mime's dynamic qualities differ from those inherent in most dances since:

> for Decroux, human beings must perpetually struggle and inevitably suffer as a result of their actions. The key themes of self-creation, rebellious and heroic action, struggling and suffering, manual labor and choice based on reason form the core of Decroux's world view, esthetic and physical technique.
>
> (Sklar 1985: 65)

Traditionally, dance explodes, mime implodes; dance moves freely through the space, mime works in place; dance is play, mime is work. Among Decroux's hundreds of explanations of basic contradictions between the two, he contended that the dancer's music remains outside, while the mime's music dwells within (enchantment).

To fully understand Decroux's relation to the "internal music" (essential to his work), we return to Copeau's consideration of Dalcroze rhythmic gymnastics as less helpful in actor training than Hébert's work. Dalcroze's students seemed dependant on audible music to support their movement, while Copeau wanted actors to respond to music heard within. This inner music appropriately portrayed thought (the music of Decroux's "thought" or "meditation" improvisation) or work, for example, the music he sang as we performed counterweight exercises and pieces based on work movements, such as the *Washerwoman* and the *Carpenter*. This "music" was a sonorous equivalent for the muscular vibrato, straining to overcome weight.

Decroux undertook to struggle against weight, matter, important ideas, human suffering, history, the actor's body, and the tragic (Promethean) cost of struggle itself.

Chapter 2 continues with a section entitled "Before Being Complete/Art Must Be." This section rebuts an open letter written to Decroux from Gaston Baty, an avant-garde stage director with whom Decroux worked in 1925, just after leaving Copeau. Baty opines that Decroux's "cutting off the theatre's right hand" does not "even offer us a body from which a limb has been severed, but instead the limb from which the body has been severed" (p. 28). Whereas Baty sees the alien arts (literature, music, stage design, etc.) as the central body of theatre, Decroux considered them simply the right hand. Decroux argued, again prefiguring Grotowski:

> I think that an art is all the richer for being poor in means. Music-hall has the maximum of means, and is poor. Statuary has the minimum of means, and is rich. I think that an art is complete only if it is partial.
>
> (p. 28)

Decroux rails against theatre which "suggest[s] the thing by the thing itself," thus disqualifying itself as art (artifice and articulation for Decroux), and continues his vivid argument:

> There an actor's weakness becomes a spectacle that hides the truth. And among these weaknesses must be counted the charm of an actress and the good looks of an actor, which cloud the judgment by erecting a noiseless barrier between the acting and the audience.
>
> (p. 29)

This theoretical basis enabled Decroux to spend sixty years in the workroom (Plate 2.2), transforming some of his students into revolutionary zealots who could only agree with their teacher that

> for an art to be, the idea of one thing must be given by another thing. Hence this paradox: an art is complete only if it is partial.

(p. 30)

WORDS IN MIME

Decroux's oft-repeated formula – rich text, poor movement, poor text, rich movement – epitomizes his ever-ambivalent relationship to text as one of the alien colonizers of the actor's theatre-homeland. For him, the word "poor" had no negative connotation. He admonished that

> for a long time yet, the Mime must abstain from slipping into works of dramatic literature and must renounce the benefits of hiding behind the names of great writers.

(p. 32)

In the following sections, Decroux discusses this delicate relationship between (appropriately and beautifully) "poor" text and correspondingly "rich" movement, and the contrary, and all of the possible combinations which make a complete theatrical event. Reading this passage reminds us that Corporeal Mime is an ideal technique for Theatre of the Absurd and other kinds of "poor" literature – alien arts which do not suck up all the oxygen in the room – which allow space for "the actor art."

CHAPTER 3: DANCE AND MIME

DECROUX INSPIRED BY AN ENEMY

In this chapter, Decroux describes two recently branded condemned men: one gagged, but his body free to move, moving in response to pain; the other bound but not gagged, shouting in response to pain. "Neither of the two criminals feels a desire to dance" Decroux concludes (p. 47). For him, both men respond as actors rather than dancers, as they are inspired by pain rather than by joyous abandon, the

Plate 2.2 Etienne Decroux ca. 1959 emphasizes a point during rehearsals in New York City. Photograph: Jerry Pantzer

usual motivation for dance. Decroux describes this essence of mime, in contrast to dance, as "mobile immobility" (p. 51).

Decroux contrasted mime's "implosion" (what Eugenio Barba calls "dynamic immobility" or "sats" in Theatre Anthropology) to dance's "explosion," and defines another essential quality of mime: smoothness "like the departure of a locomotive"; the mime "seems like a dreamed statue, which turns around for us as we would walk around it" (p. 51). These two essential qualities, "mobile immobility" and "smoothness" comprise the muscular play of Corporeal Mime – "[s]taccato and smooth; life offers us these two styles" (p. 51).

The muscular play of dance, however, he described as springing, bouncing, continuous movement. "Dance is an evasion, mime is an invasion" (p. 52), the mime "lacks lightness" and the dancer "lacks weight" (p. 56). Anticipating the argument, Decroux makes a difference between artistic dance, which has somewhat more weight and resistance – all the while remaining dance – and natural dance, typically light and rebounding.

For Decroux, Corporeal Mime epitomizes work, while dance remains synonymous with diversion:

> The dancer is not even dancing; he is danced. He transports nothing, not even his own body; he is transported by his body which is transported by dance. The worker, on the contrary, demands of himself the task that we have demanded of him.

(p. 53)

Decroux continues to set mime apart from dance by grouping it with great painting, poetry, drama, and sculpture, which primarily find subject matter in unhappiness. "Art is a lament" (p. 59) he argues.

Decroux might have made a checklist proving that mime has not just "plagiarized dance":

1   Mime prefers unhappiness as subject – dance prefers joy.
2   Mime relates to work – dance relates to play. Mime, "providing a portrait of work, and dance the portrait of dance" (p. 54).
3   Mime calculates, hesitates – dance spontaneously erupts.
4   Mime weighs – dance flies.
5   Mime implodes – dance explodes.

CHAPTER 4: MIME AND MIME

After discussing theatre and mime, and subsequently dance and mime – first showing how certain areas overlap, and then their essential difference – Decroux finally turns to mime for itself. For Decroux the body becomes

> countries and I carve out frontiers. I am reinforced by the vocabulary and I say: head, neck, chest, etc. The body is viewed in the same way by a craftsman making a string marionette, or a sculptor making an articulated model.

> (p. 70)

In establishing the primacy of trunk over face and arms, Decroux argues that the face and the arms, unhindered by fear or idleness, can react immediately in response to thought: imagine someone smiling and opening her arms to greet a friend. When will the smile die and the arm cease rising? Only, Decroux says, when the thought that impels them stops. The trunk, Decroux contends, moves with greater difficulty, and Decroux proposes a technical training that will enable the actor to respond with the trunk with as much facility as the nineteenth-century pantomime (or ordinary people in everyday life) did with face and arms.

After carving up the body, Decroux carved up the space around it, arguing for "geometrical exactness." He declared that the vertical, the horizontal, and the diagonal midway between the two exist, both in breadth and in depth, and a similar design exists on the stage floor. The actor's body and its parts may move only along these lines and planes. In short, one "must be capable of going from one point to another on a route that is a succession of simple designs" (p. 79). For Decroux, clarity, and thus legibility, meant moving one part of the body through one plane in one moment of time.

Asking the question "Does art oppress genius?" Decroux answers by saying that the technical study of Corporeal Mime, rather than limiting or sterilizing the artist's imagination, "arouses ideas sleeping in the artist" and "incite[s] him to create" (p. 90).

In defining Corporeal Mime, he rejects the words "gesture" (associated with pantomime) and "movement" (associated with dance), preferring

Etienne-Jules Marey (1830–1904), after meeting the American E. Muybridge in Paris in 1881, began experimentation with stop-action cameras. In Marey's 1882 photo, *Man in white against the first black background*, we see an unwitting depiction of Decroux's *horse walk*: the weight forward on the supporting leg, on what Decroux called the *promontory*, the free leg trailing behind, open to the side, the free foot posed on the ground with the toes pulling backward as would the bristles of a paintbrush. The face is invisible, and the body, while not nude, is completely in white and as if nude. In *Demeny wearing a black costume with white lines and points for geometric time lapse photography* (1883), we see a costume similar to those Decroux used for *Little Soldiers* (1949).

instead "attitude" and describing Corporeal Mime as a succession of attitudes. Here we see the influence of **Etienne-Jules Marey**, who took stop-action photographs which articulated movement, revealing attitudes; when reassembled and performed in quick succession by an actor, they become movement again. Decroux was fond of nineteenth-century flip-books made of still drawings or photographs through which one could quickly flip using the thumb. These books in which still images or attitudes, seen in quick succession, seemed to move, prefigured the development of cinema. Decroux said that mimes, like cinematographers, make movement with stillness.

In the section entitled "Does Art Oppress Genius" Decroux argues that rather than limiting the talented performer, a study of techniques renders his imagination more fecund. He later defines Corporeal Mime, showing its difference from pantomime, as something other than a "guessing game" which "translate[s] the plot of a spoken play into mime" (p. 93). Plot plays a small or non-existent part in most of Decroux's compositions, as it does in the work of other resolute modernists, just as figures in modern painting and melody in modern music underwent a similar sea change.

Decroux ends "Mime and Mime" reminding us of the untrustworthiness of the face and hands – "instruments of falsehood, henchmen of gossip" – to tell the truth, and contending that Corporeal Mime emulates the noble and serious themes of Hugo, Beethoven, and Michelangelo rather than entertaining the general public with comedy.

In "Introduction to a Show" Decroux confides to his imaginary audience that mime "is a sequence of present actions" which cannot suggest absent things (only words can do this); instead, in mime "the only things that do not count are facts" and the manner in which things happen takes primary focus (p. 103). In short, in Corporeal Mime "form" takes greater focus than "content," or, more exactly, form **becomes** content.

He then goes on to describe in considerable detail a mime play entitled *Little Soldiers*. He cautions us that the plot has no importance, and that "only the manner of playing conveys mysterious thoughts that words cannot express" (p. 104). How? This play uses no house curtain, all scene changes made in full view of the audience. No narrator suggests absent things, scene changes, or time changes. Actors "juggle" stools, tables, chairs, and other accessories on to and off the stage. Lighting effects do not vary. The action speeds up or slows down, but never stops until the end of the play. In one place he describes the actors as "marionettes of flesh and blood" and in another place as "warm, playful men"; in yet another, the "acrobatic tricks on the furniture make them appear to be so many clowns" – indicating a range of acting styles within the piece. In places, the piece is like "light-hearted comedy" depicting a music hall show-within-a-play; in another place, the style changes as actors "as mobile statues, act out the ballet created by the shadows of the trees" (p. 105). Actors play musical instruments and sing, alone and in chorus. While not allowing lighting changes, Decroux does not hesitate to include "Bengal lights, Greek fires, showers of sparks, entering the dance to the sound of their own explosions, which serve as drums" (p. 106). While Decroux decries music-hall entertainment in other parts of his book, here he proudly lists words copied from a music-hall poster, which qualities he integrated into *Little Soldiers*: gaiety, laughter, rhythm, dynamism, charm, emotion. Decroux writes that the piece

> holds no surprises; everything we see in it we already knew; the order of succession is predictable and the critic can notice more inventory than invention. The development is therefore not a story; it is history.

(p. 108)

Decroux combined objective and subjective mime in *Little Soldiers*.

OBJECTIVE MIME

Decroux and Barrault had earlier explored objective and subjective mime. Objective mime, useful in creating illusions, derives from the premise that the "imagined existence of an object will become real only when the muscular disturbance imposed by this object is suitably conveyed by the body of the mimer" (Barrault 1951: 27–8). Objective mime linked clearly to nineteenth-century pantomime, as it created illusions such as walking in place, walking against the wind, climbing and descending stairs, and other depictions of actions and objects in the external world. Whereas nineteenth-century pantomime, as far as we can tell, used primarily the extremities – the more easily moved face, hands, and arms – Decroux and Barrault's more muscular work created illusions with the whole body, especially the trunk – hence the name "Corporeal Mime." In the former, the body remained balanced; in the latter, weight shifted toward imbalanced precariousness.

SUBJECTIVE MIME

Barrault describes subjective mime as the "study of states of the soul translated into bodily expression. The metaphysical attitude of man in space" (Barrault 1951: 28). Whereas objective mime existed in the nineteenth century, and performers simply treated it in a different way in the twentieth, subjective mime is a purely modernist invention. It did not exist before, just as modern dance, also concerned in its way with "states of the soul translated into bodily expression," did not exist before Isadora, Ruth St Denis, and Ted Shawn. Subjective mime became an

> intoxicating study which lifts you up to the level of religious art. When we were pursuing our researches into subjective mime we felt we were drawing near to Oriental actors; we felt we were discovering all over again the plastic art of Greek tragedy.
>
> (Barrault 1951: 28)

If objective mime expressed illusions, subjective mime describes Decroux's research in mobile statuary, men in a state of beatific reflection (*songe*), and *méditation*. These areas, called "abstract" by some, Decroux considered firmly rooted in the concrete, despite appearances. Decroux, able to translate counterweights from objective to subjective mime, saw how a person carrying a physical weight resembled one carrying a metaphysical one. Here Decroux's research links to religious art, the Asian actor and Greek tragedy. Decroux and Barrault, returning to the sacred source of drama far from commercial entertainment, would have failed had they simply entertained. The struggle to return to this sacred source was modern in its rigor, its purity, and singleness of purpose.

FORM AND CONTENT IN DECROUX'S WORK

The careful observer notices neither feathers nor beak in Brancusi's sculpture, "Flight"; no content distracts from the highly refined form which evokes something akin to a soaring bird, but which also resembles a sleekly "abstract" object, an embodiment of energetic escape from gravity. In much modern art, form defines and determines content as much as the contrary. "We are not slaves of realism" Decroux thundered during rehearsals for *The Carpenter*, explaining why we did not literally recreate a carpenter's activities. Like Brancusi, Gertrude Stein, Picasso, and James Joyce, Decroux early on liberated himself from literalism.

Considering form/content as black and white leads to simplistic and un-nuanced thinking about something more correctly seen as a continuum. Along this continuum, many nuances of the form/content opposition manifest themselves. At one extreme, conventional dramaturgy defines the specific link between form and content. At other places along the continuum, however, form **creates** content. Decroux had good company (for most of his career and in most of his work) on the form end of this imaginary continuum, among other modernists, whose

> [f]ormalist or "abstract" theories of art have provided the most fundamental challenges to representational models in the modern era. Many of these theories take music (which, for obvious reasons, is hard to describe in representational terms) as the paradigm for all the arts. Formalism emphasizes the representational means and manner – the materiality and organization of the "signifier" or representational object – and de-emphasizes the other two angles of the representational triangle. The represented object may even disappear when the medium turns itself back on its own codes, engaging in self-reflexive play.
>
> (Mitchell 1995: 16)

But these experiments are fewer in theatre and film – remember Meyerhold's formalism provoked his murder! Actors, notoriously eager to attract and please audiences, seem to suffer more from Copeau's *cabotinage* (ham acting) than musicians, dancers, or visual artists.

In discussing Decroux's cubist, modernist, and often abstract pieces, we see that nineteenth-century (and even later) notions of dramaturgy as the link between content and form do not apply. The inherent problem with the defamiliarized human body in Corporeal Mime becomes, "Why don't I recognize the event?" The series of paintings by Mondrian of trees, which begins with a recognizable tree and ends (five or six studies later) in the right angles and primary colors recognized as Mondrian's signature work, exemplifies one of Decroux's ideas: the concrete flowers into the abstract. While Decroux sometimes went through that process of abstracting, he also sometimes jumped directly into right angles and primary colors through "automatic writing" (improvisations based on natural asymmetricality and the "void").

Roland Barthes wrote in his "Introduction to the Structural Analysis of Narrative":

> The function of narrative is not to "represent," it is to constitute a spectacle.... Narrative does not show, does not imitate.... "What takes place" in a narrative is from the referential (reality) point of view literally *nothing*; "what happens" is language alone, the adventure of language, the unceasing celebration of its coming.
>
> (quoted in White 1987: 37)

Decroux would agree, and by replacing the word "narrative" with the words "Corporeal Mime" we have a perfectly Decrousian paragraph:

> The function of Corporeal Mime is not to "represent," it is to constitute a spectacle.... Corporeal Mime does not show, does not imitate.... "What takes place" in Corporeal Mime is from the referential (reality) point of view literally *nothing*; "what happens" is Mime alone, the adventure of Mime, the unceasing celebration of its coming.

For Barthes, like Decroux, "the way of saying is all-important, the thing said banal to the point of non-existence" (Thody 1977: 17).

> The *haïku* is able, by a whole technique, by what is even a metric code, to make the signified – what is meant – disappear. All that remains is a thin cloud of signifier. And it is at that very moment, it seems, that, by a final twist, the *haïku* takes on the mask of the legible, and copies, while nevertheless depriving them of all *reference*, the attributes of the "good" (literary) message: clarity, simplicity, elegance, delicacy.
>
> (Thody 1977: 185)

Decroux explains that his primary interest is in the creation of a style of acting and not storytelling; to undertake storytelling, he would use words, better adapted to the task than Corporeal Mime.

In "Prologue for *Le Toréador*," Decroux describes his life-long antipathy for the audience, comparing the actor to the toreador, the audience to a bull; in order to succeed, the actor must thrust his sword into the audience's "tendon of irony." This image refers to Decroux's desire to attract an audience with open, child-like eyes, ready to see the wonders he saw, rather than a sophisticated adult audience saturated in wit and irony, which would blind them to his poetry.

In "The Garden of the Fine Arts is not a Vegetable Garden," Decroux continues the form/content debate, arguing that "The manner in which one gives/is worth more than what one gives" (p. 118). When Decroux writes "Style is a story" he says "Form creates content" in a way that sets him radically apart from any other theatre-maker of the twentieth century. These formalistic leanings explain his isolation, and the time it has taken for him to gain recognition among his less controversial peers – Meyerhold, for example, whose less abstract movement studies often served the playwright.

In the chapter entitled "Teaching," Decroux discusses a "Justification for a corporeal mime class in a school for actors." Here he obfuscates; he himself rarely taught in a traditional acting school, and when he did, he did not want to create better actors for the theatre as it existed. His thinly veiled intention, to destroy the traditional theatre, could make way for his revolutionary vision known as Corporeal Mime.

He again argues for the supremacy of the trunk over the arms and hands, and discusses kinds of movement and walking which will not distract from text. This explanation becomes part of his ruse, as he refused to give text the upper hand and would prefer to, most of the time, discuss kinds of text which would not interfere with movement rather than the contrary.

Decroux then discusses two kinds of comedy: one which diminishes, and makes fun of people's diminishing energy as they age – a kind of dirty comedy; the other, a hypertrophy of the beautiful, an excess of energy, a beautiful comedy. The first requires no special training; Corporeal Mime exemplifies the second, fraught with difficult balance.

In the section entitled "To the Spectators at Our School" a vista opens before us of a man who considered the work in the classroom more important than performance – indeed, for whom the work in the classroom *became* a kind of performance, so much so that, during one period, he issued tickets to spectators to attend class on Thursdays from 5 until 8 p.m. According to his description, the lessons they would observe would include technical work on figures as well as improvisation, all commented upon by Mr Decroux himself, the chief researcher, always observing closely and commenting in depth on the students' work.

One of the gems of this chapter is Decroux's remark:

> If manners are engendered by feelings, is it not necessary to think that feelings, in their turn, are engendered by manners? If so, the study of good manners must produce good feelings.

(p. 134)

Decroux often quoted Pascal's reflection: "If you would believe, pray" to reinforce an idea which François Delsarte, Decroux's nineteenth-century forbear, would have seconded. Decroux makes his position clear in the age-old chicken-egg debate as to whether emotion begets form or form begets emotion.

In "Servitude Without Greatness," Decroux pokes scathing fun at the actor's condition, making clear the impossibility of creating art in the world he describes where actors are constantly looking for work; auditioning and interviewing with disorganized, overwrought, fickle, and pretentious directors; subjected to scenery, costumes, and make-up which prevent the actor from doing his job; oppressed by type-casting. In short, the commercial actor's lot, as described by Decroux in 1943, has not greatly changed today, except in those comparatively few theatres rooted in an ideological basis rather than a commercial one.

In "For Better and For Worse," the last section of the last chapter in the book, Decroux shows his hand. He tells us straight out what he has more or less intimated from the start: "Western theatre is not an art. But it is an entertainment." Decroux intended to remedy this, creating – in place of commercial entertainment based on literature, personality, and type-casting – an "actor art" ruled by articulation and artifice. Decroux knew the difficulty well: that "[t]he mime's arrival upon the stage of the speaking actor can destroy the entertainment without having created the art" (p. 149).

Decroux admits that somehow theatre carries on, despite actors' deficiencies and inadequate training, and these lacks are compensated for by reliance upon furniture and scenery; reliance upon costumes; reliance upon properties; reliance upon lighting; and "reliance upon plays that can be staged without artists trained in the use of the body" – in other words, reliance upon literature.

The chapter ends with this provocative sentence: "Mime invites the actor to painstaking studies so that he may rise to the rank of non-entity." Decroux had another way of saying the same thing: "You must master movement so that you can stand completely still on stage without provoking comment." In short, completely mastered mime becomes invisible in the work of the orthodox actor.

In a last section called "Regrets," added to the American edition, Decroux mentions two "brothers": Jean-Georges Noverre (1727–1810) and Kurt Joss (1901–79).

Noverre advanced court dances toward dramatic ballet with the "pas d'action," non-decorative movement which carried dramatic freight. He also adapted costumes to allow greater mobility for the dancer, and eliminated leather masks. Removing speech and song, he made dance the primary art in a "ballet d'action" served by music, drama, costume, and design, and not dominated by them.

German choreographer Kurt Joss' signature ballet, *The Green Table*, won an important choreographic prize in Paris in July 1932, the year of its creation, when Decroux probably saw it. A tantalizing mixture of drama – abstracted design (archetypes in characterization), and militant politics – *The Green Table* marked Decroux, who, thirty years later, still spoke of it fondly.

Decroux ends his text with a few lines on Charlie Chaplin, "the name of the gymnast, of the artist and of the citizen whose soul, assuredly, transcends his craft" (p. 154). These words say a great deal about

Decroux's ideal actor. First, the actor should possess a hard-won and well-honed craft, and second he must transcend it, using it to express the Promethean struggle of life.

NOTE

1 All references in this chapter are to Etienne Decroux's *Words on Mime* (1985) unless otherwise indicated.

DECROUX AS DIRECTOR/CREATOR

How did Decroux make a performance?

BANISHING TEXT

Most directors ask: "What play shall I produce?" or "What work of literature shall I adapt for the stage?" Their primary job becomes the interpretation or elaboration of that text. Decroux, who wanted to exile literature from the theatre to develop exclusively the "actor art," contrarily began with the actor on a bare stage. With the exception of two plays he prepared in 1941, in a failed attempt to gain government subsidy (Benheïm 2003: 252), Decroux always began without text. The author, he contended, lived in a different world, a "sitting down world," while the actor inhabited a "standing up world." The limited expectations of the former could only inhibit the latter. While the author worked exclusively with words, the actor acts with words, without them, or, usually, in spite of them.

We established in previous chapters that Decroux wanted to exile what he called the "alien arts" from the theatre; one could say that he wanted to send the author further away than any of the other theatre collaborators, for the author had become for Decroux the theatre's chief oppressor or colonizer. When we speak of Etienne Decroux as a twentieth-century theatre revolutionary, we may note that in that select company, he (and Jacques Lecoq) alone proposed a paradigm shift which questioned theatre's historically established relationship with text.

Only during the heyday of Commedia dell'arte, he found, had Western actors broken free of the author's chains. Decroux's job became proclaiming the actor's freedom for our time.

MAKING PERFORMANCES FROM IMPROVISATION

Without text, how did Decroux begin to create a theatre piece? With the actor's collaboration he initiated a series of guided improvisations which he described as a "petri dish" (Decroux 2003: 59). He allowed the actor's random or unconscious movements to grow, and subsequently edited and built upon this growth, or expunged it and began afresh. Corinne Soum describes improvising as the first steps toward creation of a piece with Decroux this way:

> From time to time Decroux conjured up the traces of a theme to help us, but more often threw at me, with a joyous voice, "Go on, do something!" Or he declared, with a serious voice, "It's beautiful to be mystical" or yet again "This morning I saw a sparrow taking a bath." Out of the question, of course, to "mime" these statements, but one had to use them as a kind of terrain of sensations, a storehouse of impressions.
>
> (Soum 1999: 62–3)

Soum reminds us that it was never a question of literally reproducing Decroux's remarks, but instead of using these "traces of a theme" as a metaphorical springboard to suggest a way of moving through space, a way of being in space, that might eventually result in the creation of a composition.

In my work with him, Decroux told me to follow "naturally asymmetrical tendencies," to lean in whatever direction my body wanted to go on that particular day, and to continue until I met an exterior limitation (the wall, the floor) or an internal one (e.g. the knee will only bend so far; the arm has raised to its maximum). Along the way, he wanted me to begin to hear what he described as an "internal music," a sort of nonrhythmic series of sounds – more vibrations, really – that resembled articulated speech. Since I could not hear them at first, he sang – sometimes quite forcefully – what they sounded like to him. When improvising successfully, the actor's body entered a special world, a metaphorical one, in which it created these inaudible but very real, internal sounds (like depth-charges exploding in the psyche's undersea) and followed their reverberations simultaneously.

If the reader has trouble envisioning what kinds of movements the body as a "consequence and prolongation of thought" (Soum 1999: 62) might make, rest assured that his students found it equally difficult. But after some time – more or less time depending upon the aptitude of the improviser for nonlinear understanding – the quotidian movements of a person deeply lost in thought became a possible terrain on which to build. These movements (because of their ordinariness), if made in public, might not shock an observer. But the actor's training in Corporeal Mime vocabulary allowed him to continue certain lines of force (leaning pensively forward; turning suddenly away as if repelled by an idea) into a logically satisfying configuration of movements which had departed significantly, yet logically, from their original quotidian source.

Every day for most of 1970, Zoe Noys Maistre and I stood in front of Decroux and improvised for the better part of an hour. He offered suggestions, interrupting our attempts with praise or with censure, but guided us mostly with the sheer silent power of his presence and his piercing regard. One had the feeling one had never really been seen before. Little sequences, more or less complete in themselves, figures based on protecting, cradling, being attracted to, or pushing away from, slowly emerged from these improvisations. (Years later I would realize that the attraction, repulsion, or remaining still we manifested in this duet were but smaller versions – but not necessarily less powerful ones – of the counterweights manifested in *The Carpenter* or *The Washerwoman*.) We rehearsed these figures – to which he gave poetic and evocative titles like "rising sap" or "sunshine on your back" – in different orders until he finally settled upon an order he preferred. Decroux, who never knew what he was looking for until he found it, encapsulated his way of creating a piece through improvisation this way:

> First, one must improvise without even knowing the theme upon which one is improvising.
>
> Thus, one finds a theme, then a second, then a third.
>
> You must therefore move in order to think.
>
> In placing in a logical order the ideas one finds in moving, a play composes itself without words ever breaking the silence.
>
> We find the usefulness of words by doing without them.
>
> (Decroux 1950: 7)

This method of letting the "play compose itself" required of both director and actors patience and time; one could not feel hurried, as one had to surrender completely to the process. Anything less would sabotage it. He often said "patience is a long passion" to fortify us when we tired (he never seemed to), or told the humorous story of a British gentlemen who says to his driver: "Go slowly, we're late!" Decroux's themes were never literary ideas but always poetic and metaphoric physical explorations – discoveries of the way the body related to space and to other bodies. The "how" became more important than the "what" and, in fact, the "how" became the "what."

As a way to explain his method of working, Decroux told a story about a necklace of potatoes. He said: If I give you a string of potatoes and ask you to imagine a string of pearls, you might have some difficulty. But if I give you one pearl, and ask you to imagine a necklace of them, you will have a better chance. Decroux liked to work on individual pearls (figures or phrases) for a sometimes frustratingly long (for the actor) time. Polishing, changing, revising, refining, smoothing – and then he moved reluctantly on to another pearl, and another; finally he could string these carefully crafted phrases into a felicitous order. He often called his work "jewelry making." Before he could string the necklace, however, the actors had sometimes left the school, either out of a desire (premature in Decroux's opinion) to perform, or through the material necessity to do something that could eventually earn them a living. Decroux took refuge from this constant source of disappointment by redoubling his efforts to create something beautiful and lasting; somehow, he finally succeeded on his own terms.

While Decroux foresaw the eventual reintegration of text into the theatrical event, he thought this could happen only after the actor had expelled "colonizers" from other fields; his own work (with few exceptions), however, did not use text, even in a secondary role, and he warned his students from taking shelter under great literary names.

DECROUX'S ACTOR

Decroux could not direct ordinary actors who had not undergone rigorous and transformative training in Corporeal Mime which, during his own lifetime, usually only he could provide. Hence as we examine Decroux the director, inevitably we see Decroux the teacher/creator. From this already small group of trained performers, Decroux carefully selected individuals whom he would trust with his work, as he would not, and could not, work on pieces with just any one of his students. He had to feel empathy, a seriousness of purpose, a certain possibility in the actor. Being asked to rehearse with him outside of regular class hours was an honor, usually bestowed upon his teaching assistants only, but sometimes on a special few others for whom he felt a certain regard.

Nicole Pinaud, one of the last to work with him in this special way, describes the symbiotic relationship between Decroux and the actor:

> I think I was like all those who lent their bodies to him to create – unconscious matter which corresponded to his universe. But he also corresponded to mine. In that, he was not only a Pygmalion, he also revealed my own dreams to me.
>
> There was an echo, resonance between us. Or love.
>
> (Pinaud 2003: 510–11)

Marcel Marceau, who worked with Decroux just after World War II, spoke poignantly, in an interview he gave on the occasion of Decroux's death in 1991, of the "kind of deep friendship based on mutual respect . . . . I had [for him] a kind of spiritual love" (Marceau 1991: 12). And while not every actor working with Decroux felt what Pinaud and Marceau describe as love, every one whom I have met has described it as something as strong as love.

FUNDING FOR PERFORMANCES

How could Decroux afford to create such labor-intensive theatre and never sell it to a paying public? The cost of Decroux's lessons, already the least expensive in Paris, he diminished or completely waived if one became his teaching assistant, translator, or worked with him on a performance. The student actor, who did not pay with money, had to pay daily in strict attendance and unquestioning devotion to the requirements of the work, including what could seem like the director's arbitrary whims – and this not for a month or two only, but for a period of years.

Decroux, who never took a penny of subsidy of any kind, underwrote his own work in this way. From 1960 onward, he taught in the basement of his own small house and lived extremely modestly. He had some income from retirement pensions as well as rental income from a small apartment and a café at the same address as his house. He took no vacations, never owned a car, never flew in an airplane, and rarely ate in a restaurant; books were his only luxury. In the house, the basement work room and Decroux's study took primary focus – the miniature kitchen, bath, bedroom, and upstairs changing room seemed afterthoughts. He produced his private art to please himself and a few others and, like a Renaissance prince, but on a miniature scale, he subsidized it from his own funds. As Eugenio Barba once said, Decroux succeeded in "carving out an island of freedom" which was small in scale yet provided him the liberty to create.

His actors, too, had to subsidize their work, from which they never earned money even if they paid him no tuition. They supported themselves mostly with menial jobs – teaching English, baby-sitting – or they received money from parents.

From 1960 onward, he presented performances almost exclusively in his basement classroom which he had equipped with one theatrical light, curtains at one end of the small space, and folding canvas stools for the audience. He charged no admission and did no publicity for his presentations, although he sometimes sent postcards to friends inviting them to the readings he gave of Victor Hugo or Baudelaire. He had managed to reduce the theatrical event to its basic elements. It became, in his vision of it, an extremely costly gift given to a precious few.

Audience members for mime presentations or readings might include the concierge and her bus-driver husband, former and current students, and long-time friends of Monsieur and Madame Decroux – but never more than twenty altogether.

THE OTHER "ALIEN ARTS"

Along with text, Decroux banished what he called "artistic lighting" in favor of the bright, white, unchanging light one would find in open air performances. He insisted that the actor must do the work – the phrasing and changes in focus – which "artistic lighting" often accomplishes. He also dismissed costumes, preferring at first an almost nude body, and later simple tights and leotards (which he found made the body more "nude" than the truly nude body which, because of its imperfections, attracted undue attention). Masks or veiled faces, important in an early phase of his work, almost completely disappeared (with some exceptions we will examine later). He used simple costumes and some make-up rarely, as in a production like *The Little Soldiers*, but they never figured prominently in his work.

Decroux at first adamantly refused music as well, later reversing his opinion and welcoming it as the one necessary alien art, an "alcohol" which could turn the fruit juice of life into an exquisite liquor of art.

THE MOVEMENT ITSELF: COUNTERWEIGHTS

Now that we have seen what Decroux's work excluded and the unique context in which he created and performed it, what *was* it?

He created two works in the early days of his career which he continued to perfect until the end of his life, *The Carpenter* and *The Washing* (the title changed to *The Washerwoman* when he designed the completely white costume for my 1973 version). While other works appeared and disappeared, he returned periodically to these touch-stones, part of the category of work he entitled Artisan Life (a subcate-gory of Man of Sport). Decroux describes this historical period as one in which man had no extra-animal motor, and had to become skilled and agile in order to accomplish his work. For Decroux, this period represented a kind of paradise lost, a golden age before human bodies atrophied from lack of use, or became deformed from imbalanced and stressful labor. Decroux contrasted the echoes of counterweights we use today with daily use of counterweights in the past, or as he employed them in *The Carpenter* and *The Washerwoman*:

> In life we make certain expressive gestures that complete our words, or augment their force. We do them with such spontaneity that they must be really ancient. I believe that one of the dominant things in prehistoric man was the [use of] counterweights. It was almost his daily regimen. And the use of counterweights as a dominant activity lasted well after the prehis-toric period with the slaves of antiquity, the serfs of the Middle Ages or with the artisan.
>
> (Decroux 2003: 130)

Decroux often said that bodily counterweights became necessary for workers who did not possess great innate strength. Both pieces require counterweights, their work revealing and exulting in them in their myriad forms. Decroux devised the exercises "doing away with the support," "jumping to fall on the head," "the wool-carding machine," and "reestablishment of two elements on the oblique" (or "*sissonne*") to describe specific kinds of counterweights used in work-based figures and etudes.

1   *Doing away with the support*: The actor, quickly retreating his leg and foot, falls upon the object he wishes to move with his upper body. The leg that remains fixed to the ground becomes the fixed point against which the body transforms vertical (falling) movement into horizontal (pushing) movement. The actor is able to pull instead of push by placing the object on the other side of the fulcrum.

2   *Jumping to fall on the head*: In this counterweight, the actor jumps into the air, and in falling to the ground, the body's weight translates from a vertical fall to a horizontal push around the central axle (fulcrum point) in the pelvis.

3   *The wool-carding machine*: (Decroux saw one in his early adulthood, and the image stayed with him, as this machine has two curved forks, which resemble the arc the body forms and traces in the eponymous exercise). The previous two counterweights push or pull along the horizontal line, whereas the wool-carding machine lifts weight. The idea suggested by this machine places the body in an arc; when the chord of the arc moves backward around a fixed central point (a fulcrum), the lifting activity occurs.

4   *Reestablishment of two elements on the oblique* (*sissonne*): This counterweight forms the basis of the most basic work: displacement in walking. The legs straighten to reestablish. If they do so vertically, the person remains in place, able only to take fruit from trees by jumping. But in order to go to the next tree, the person must reestablish on the oblique line, provoking a small fall, and then again; the repetition, according to Decroux, becomes walking. Decroux often quoted Charles Gide: "Production comes down to displacement" (Decroux 1985: 109).

These counterweights move the work from the periphery (hands) to the center of the actor's body, three inches below the navel. Even if the hands did sometimes of necessity occupy space away from the center of the body, they needed strong energetic links to that center. While the hands hold the tool – often close to the center of the body – the body does the work. Counterweights completely alter the intracorporeal and interspatial relationships between center and surface. (According to Decroux, a pantomime might begin with the surface – the tip of the iceberg – and never work into the center. Most importantly, the pantomime runs the risk of not having a continuous inner connection from hands to the center through imagined energetic links.)

THE DYNAMIC CONSTRUCTION – "DYNAMO-RHYTHM"

A verbal description, even accompanied by drawings, cannot give the reader any idea of the rhythmic complexity of *The Carpenter* and *The Washerwoman*; in Decroux's mind, Corporeal Mime performances had to satisfy the audience through phrasing, as poetry or music do. He invented the word *dynamo-rhythm* to describe a combination of three elements: trajectory of the movement; its speed; and its weight – the resistance it met when moving through space. He counted on dynamo-rhythm to "slap the audience to keep them awake." For example, whenever the actor moved an arm along a predetermined pathway, it infrequently reached its final destination, since Decroux said that one must anticipate the audience's boredom and shift suddenly to the next movement before their attention strayed. This was called "killing the gesture before it dies." As the actor's arm moved more than halfway toward its destination, he "killed" the gesture before it – and the audience's attention – died, "editing out" its completion, splicing in, without transition, the next activity.

This cubistic cutting and shaping of activity and sequence gave the compositions a sometimes shattered, nervous, and jittery surface, or, contrastingly, sometimes a voluminous surface, when the movements became rounder and slower. The Corporeal Mime might accomplish a grouping of four or five smaller movements with a percussive and implosive rhythm, or a larger movement with a steady slow-motion quality; or surprisingly, he might perform these movements with their opposite dynamo-rhythm. Decroux constantly refined qualities of a composition – soft or hard, heavy or light, with or without attack, accelerating or decelerating – as he often brought an improvement to the shape of the movement. Sirlei Alaniz describes Decroux's approach to dynamo-rhythm this way:

> Corporeal mime never imposes a metrical rhythmic structure. Historically, it is founded on rhythms of work, of crafts, of physical actions of man in his

> environment. These include accelerations, pauses, quick changes of
> movement, and slowing down, which are necessities.
>
> (Alaniz 2004: 19)

These work movements led often to more subjective moments, moments of pure acting, which alternated with work:

> It's the rhythm of man who works, who thinks, and who, while thinking,
> doubts, stops, speeds up, resists, gives space for the unexpected, never
> follows predictable cadences.
>
> (Alaniz 2004: 20)

Decroux evolved a vast number of what he called "causalities" – ways of defining how a movement began (e.g. imperceptibly, as when triggered by an electric eye; brusquely, as when un-sticking from a surface; or as the consequence of another body part beginning the movement beforehand and pulling or pushing the second part). He also defined ways of placing accents within the trajectory of a movement (accelerations, decelerations, or small stops or "tocs" embedded in the movement), and defined ways of ending a movement – for example, suddenly, as when hitting a large immovable object; or with a light internal "toc" which marked its arrival at an imaginary finish line.

Of causalities Decroux once said: "When I was young I thought causalities could replace plot completely." He often gave them poetic names which helped the actor to play them imaginatively: snail's antennae, tug-boat, spider web, electric eye, etc.

The Corporeal Mime, always engaged in a struggle with weight and inertia (his own; that of the tools he manipulated; that of the matter he struggled to shape; that of his own or another's thought), constantly pushes, pulls, carves, and twists both his own body and the matter he manipulates, as one mirrors the other.

We might imagine the Corporeal Mime, trained to continue or to cut lines of force, as a person attached to the earth with invisible elastic bands of variable resistance. Moving his hand through space to pick up a glass of water, moving a foot forward in order to walk, turning the head quickly or slowly – all these quotidian movements require more energy, more struggle, and hence have higher dramatic value than their equivalents in real life. The Corporeal Mime constantly negotiates these difficulties, plays with these variable weights and resistances, desiring greatly the culmination of the task. Sometimes it seems the Corporeal Mime moves through different poetic zones, with differing temperatures, or through imaginary substances, like molasses or across a silk surface. When the "how" becomes this interesting, the "what" certainly has to take second place.

MATERIAL ACTIONS SUGGEST MENTAL STATES

In the contrasting activities of *The Carpenter* and *The Washerwoman*, the actor's body takes on the qualities of the objects used and the activities mimed. Working with wood differs fundamentally from working with cloth and, while the counterweights used in each piece may resemble each other, each study requires a different agility and movement quality. The actor, in learning to play these roles, schools his body in a wide range of dynamo-rhythm which suggests an equally wide range of emotions or states of thought. For Decroux, the material formed the basis of everything else: thought, spirit, emotion, dreams. He often said "I am what you could call a spiritual-materialist. That's to say the spiritual influences me when it gives form to the material" (Decroux 2003: 57).

And so the exploration of various kinds of matter – in different situations, with different weights – became a primary focus of his work.

> Not everything is round, but everything weighs. Not everything is pointed, but everything weighs. Not everything is hot, but everything weighs. Not everything is tender, but everything weighs. And it's astonishing that when I realized that everything weighed, the idea didn't come to me to rely on the simple fact that the earth attracts bodies and it's because the earth attracts bodies that everything weighs. You see the importance of what we call counterweights.
>
> (Decroux 2003: 131)

The constant struggle with weight lies at the heart of each one of Decroux's compositions, perhaps none more so than *The Carpenter* and *The Washerwoman*, where it begins to take on metaphorical and symbolic connotations and one can clearly see the relationship between dynamo-rhythm and states of thought.

> Basically, when man thinks, he struggles against ideas, like we struggle
> against the material. Because we don't see ideas, because we don't see
> thoughts, because we don't have a direct hold on thought, the best thing is
> to do to a material job that implies intelligence and of which the gestures
> are like echoes of our intelligence.
>
> (Decroux 2003: 77)

As far as I can tell, abstract mime never existed before the twentieth century, before Decroux invented it. His study of weights and qualities, counterweights and dynamo-rhythm took the actor into the realm of struggle – not only with real objects, but also with thought, into the world of metaphysical counterweights and abstract mime.

Thus, his work differed radically from his nineteenth-century predecessors and his early twentieth-century contemporaries, who began in quite different ways and arrived in quite different places. Nineteenth-century pantomime told a preexisting linear, anecdotal story but replaced words with gestures. Far on the other end of the spectrum, Oskar Schlemmer's (1888–1943) Bauhaus experiments in three-dimensional moving constructivist images used costumes and masks that severely limited the actor's movements while simultaneously creating unforgettably beautiful photographs. While pantomime was about storytelling, Schlemmer's work was about exploring moving images in space, and seems to have had little dramatic weight or resistance – none of Decroux's counterweights or dynamo-rhythm. Decroux differed as well from Russian director Vsevolod Meyerhold (1874–1940), whose movement études served to illustrate or extend a text into performance, and, without the playwright, existed only as classroom exercises.

THE CARPENTER

In his book *Emile*, Jean-Jacques Rousseau selected carpentry as the profession of his ideal son. (This fact, however, hardly counts as a literary antecedent as Decroux said he read this book only after having begun work on his fifty-year project [Decroux 2003: 76].) Decroux spoke at length about why the Carpenter assumed such tremendous proportions in his own imagination: the carpenter who fells the tree, pulls it to his atelier, removes the bark, saws the wood into rough planks, imagines and draws an object he wishes to produce, cuts the planks into smaller pieces, joins individual elements into a whole, sanding and applying the appropriate finish to a utilitarian object.

> The carpenter has contact with wood, which is a beautiful material, a friendly material, an almost living material. The carpenter is a man who knows botany a little. He has to distinguish among trees; the trees have their specificities. When it's about building furniture, some of them, like the ash, are a little too flexible. He also has to know how wood should be treated, because he is going to need to let it dry a long time and he is going to bend it. What a story! There's no world like that of the carpenter. Having seen how this activity is general, how it is dramatic, because it deals with all the moral phenomena – hesitation, confidence, retrospective examination – has he made a mistake or not? Should he risk it? – we are necessarily disposed to consider it a beautiful subject.
>
> (Decroux 2003: 76)

A chair, a desk or a building, Decroux said, does not signify a thing, it *is* that thing. Corporeal mimes do not *pretend*, Madame Decroux reminded me, as I passed through the kitchen one day, that they *do*. One could not overstate Decroux's insistence that thought manifests itself in matter, that the thinker should not remain a talking head but become instead a sort of dancing philosopher. The Carpenter made his thought visible.

> So, precision, minutia, hard work: that's a complete man. We have to ask ourselves what's missing. It's the flowering of all human faculties, and as Jean Jacques Rousseau observed, it's a clean job.
>
> (Decroux 2003: 76)

As we see in the first paragraphs of this chapter, improvisation played a key role in the creation of most of Decroux's works. In the case of *The Carpenter* and *The Washerwoman*, however, Decroux was reconstructing pieces he had first made in the 1930s and had subsequently revived several times. As an actor I could suggest solutions to problems we encountered along the way, and surely my limitations or abilities shaped the version we created. But the sequence and basic scheme of the work remained unchanged from previous versions.

What happens in *The Carpenter*? Without plot or anecdote, a mere succession of actions remains. Traditional suspense – "What will happen next?" – does not manifest itself across the performance as a whole;

rather, suspense of a different sort exists within the performance of each action, in the moments of pause, weight, resistance, hesitation, and surprise before the Carpenter begins or completes an action or a gesture (see Plates 3.1 and 3.2). The "what" becomes unimportant as the "how" becomes all-important; an open spectator's focus shifts from story to actor, from plot to presence. He said of the Carpenter's work: "It's almost abstract. It's like a perfume coming from a concrete action" (Soum 1999: 18). Often he reminded his students that the abstract was the flower of the concrete. The Carpenter is a generality, he said, almost an abstraction:

> We've encountered *a* horse, but not *the* horse. We've never seen *the* Frenchman, we've seen *a* Frenchman. And it's like that with everything. We've never seen *the* carpenter, either.
>
> (Decroux 2003: 77)

Decidedly antirealistic in his conception of theatre, Decroux had worked with film director Pierre Prévert and stage director and author Antonin Artaud (1898–1948), both of whom also were antirealistic in their approaches. He observed that

> there are people in this vast movement who are anti-realistic in literature, painting, and sculpture, but when it comes to the actor – finished! They fall back into a kind of realism which reminds us of the period of Antoine and Stanislavsky.
>
> (Decroux 2003: 189)

Decroux's compositions, by not "falling back into a kind of realism," risked alienating audiences as they pushed the limits of theatre.

> There are people who are happy to see a body that moves without knowing what it means. Then, there are others who aren't interested by that. You can't make concessions in this sphere.
>
> (Decroux 2003: 92)

THE CARPENTER: THE "WHAT"

1   Introduction. The person becomes an actor, who in turn becomes a carpenter.

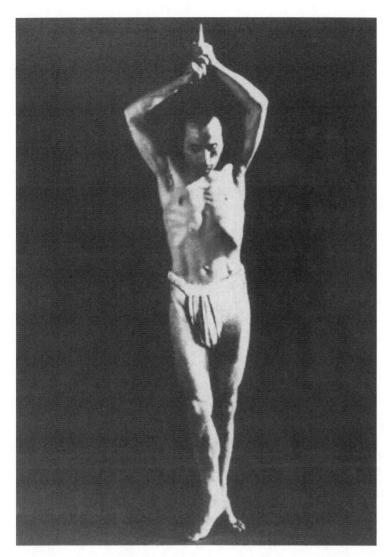

Plate 3.1 Etienne Decroux in *The Carpenter* ca. 1950. Here the Carpenter holds the screwdriver aloft prior to placing it in the tool box. Note the wrists resisting the forearms, and the arms resisting the shoulders, to create an energetic design based on opposition. Photograph: Gaston

Plate 3.2 Steven Wasson in *The Carpenter*, 1994. Wasson studied with Decroux from 1980 to 1984, and served as his teaching assistant. With Corinne Soum he directs the Théâtre de l'Ange Fou and a corporeal mime school in London. Photograph: Lionel Forneaux

2   He planes a plank of wood and puts the plane away.
3   He reaches for a compass, engraves a circle into the wood and puts the compass away.
4   He reaches up to a shelf and takes down a jar. After unscrewing the jar lid, he places it on the shelf. He searches in the jar for a screw of just the right size, finds it, and returns the jar to the shelf. He holds the screw vertical in relation to the plank of wood, looks for and finds a hammer, and gives the screw a light tap which plants its tip into the wood. He looks for and finds a screwdriver which he uses to tighten the screw. At one point during this activity, thinking he hears his wife (the Washerwoman) call to him, he looks over his shoulder but decides he was mistaken. He returns to his work, completes it, and returns the screwdriver to the tool box.
5   He looks for and finds a pencil stuck behind his right ear. He takes it out and places its point on the surface of the plank. He traces a figure eight on the wood plank. He puts the pencil back behind his ear.
6   He takes a box of gouges from the shelf. He looks into the box to find just the right gouge. He takes it out and tests its sharpness. When satisfied it will do the job, he begins to gouge the wood. When finished with this activity, he sees a knothole in the wood, which he removes with the gouge. He leaves the gouge stuck in the wood.
7   To finish, he brushes the sweat from his forehead, and caresses the wood.

THE CARPENTER: THE "HOW"

This sequence is hardly "realistic," as one would end up with a plank which had a circle traced on it, a screw planted in the middle of it, and bits of wood gouged out of it (an abstract sculpture?). Decroux obviously ordered these activities for other than literal reasons. The play is about the movements themselves, and their ordinarily hidden life.

> The Carpenter, in particular, made certain gestures with a certain violence, and, like [things moving] in water, these gestures call out for continuation. In practical, everyday life, the gesture is stopped. We have the impression that actions are like hairs – they ask to grow, but social life, or even other necessities, oblige you to cut them close to the head. So close that we don't

understand the whole truth, all the "power" of things. We see what they are, but not what they want to be. So, in *The Carpenter*, lots of movements are the continuation of something that, of habit, is normally cut with social scissors.

(Decroux 2003: 78)

A note on the method

At the start of the seven-minute piece, the person first transforms himself into an actor, then into a character, and subsequently the character transforms matter. Dealing with the question of characterization: the actor may embody the ideal of a carpenter, but does not attempt to become a specific carpenter of a specific age who wants something in Stanislavskian terms. Only once in four years did Decroux offer any personal information about the Carpenter, and he did so almost jokingly. He told me that the Carpenter married the Washerwoman, and they lived in the south of France, where the sun shone more frequently than in Paris, in a cottage surrounded by fields of lavender. Resistance posed by the inertia of his own body; challenges posed by the picture inside his head of the object he wishes to create; the weight and resistance of the materials with which he works – the person-as-actor-as-carpenter's work consists of overcoming these obstacles, rather than psychological ones. Decroux did not believe in psychology or psychiatry – he believed only in thought made visible through action.

Decroux would have agreed with Lecoq that all acting becomes pushing and pulling (I pull you toward me, I push you from me); the Carpenter pushes and pulls against great physical and spiritual weights. The Carpenter is Decroux's Hamlet (another character from an age before psychology), embodying the pause, weight, resistance, hesitation, and surprise we find between and among the ellipsis points of "to be . . . or not to be."

1 The person becomes the actor who becomes the character

A lone person, dressed in tights and a leotard, sits on an ordinary white wooden kitchen chair, downstage left, facing upstage. He (a woman could just as easily play the role) is himself, having "slept well or poorly, having had a good breakfast or not," as Decroux said. He begins by shifting his weight forward, and as he stands on his right foot he swings his left foot forward and walks two or three steps, stopping with heels together and feet slightly turned out. As right heel touches left ankle, a causality creates a kind of current which passes through the body, straightening up the body more, changing it from person into actor.

No longer himself, but now an actor, he walks upstage three steps (a gliding, idealized walk which took months to learn), turns an eighth of a turn toward the back corner, takes another step, and then shifts again one quarter of a turn toward the front corner. While remaining standing, he "wilts" and his center of gravity falls backward, then surges forward again and moves directly front to center stage. These forward surges and relaxations backward are microcosmic portraits of the actor's giving in to, and then overcoming inertia and fatigue, preparing, sometimes reluctantly, to assume the role.

As he opens an imaginary curtain and passes through, he completes the transformation from actor to character. An audience member would not necessarily recognize this gesture of opening a curtain (years later I saw similar moments when Balinese and Khatakhali actors appeared from behind curtains), or the concrete basis of any of the subsequent gestures, no matter how clearly based on real models. A pantomine fails if the audience does not understand the literal meaning of his gestures; Decroux, on the other hand, never intended the audience to understand literally any of his gestures.

The actor's weight falls downward (from raised heels to a small, percussive touching of the joined heels on the stage floor), and in that second he becomes The Carpenter and his hands, in resonance from the shock of heels touching stage floor, define the first tool, the plane.

2 The plane

The Carpenter, now downstage center, planes an imaginary plank of wood in various ways, using an old-fashioned plane – a long, thin, rectangular wooden box, containing a sharpened blade which can be adjusted to protrude from the box more or less, thereby determining the amount of wood which will be shaved off on each pass. The Carpenter's whole body simplifies and amplifies the gesture, revealing the importance of counterweights – only the whole body can accomplish the work, the hands and arms do not have the strength to do it on their own.

In planing the wood, the head and chest enter into a left/left/front design (bust rotated left, inclined left, inclined forward). When the actual work of planing takes place – when the blade in the plane cuts into the wood – an imaginary plumb line (attached to the center of the actor's body) moves forward to traverse the left ankle. If the plumb line falls short of the ankle, no real physical work seems to have taken place. One finds this engaged attitude, forward gravity, in classical sculpture and in the activities of manual laborers. As the Carpenter prepares to plane, he "jumps to fall on his head." In this movement, the body gathers downward momentum, which is then diverted to provide the main force behind the planing. He works first in profile to the audience – as if carved into the surface of a medallion – and later, body facing the audience, as he planes a different part of the wood.

At a certain moment, the plane encounters a knothole, on which the blade of the plane catches. This catching (like other added bits of resistance we will see later – the rusty compass, the stuck cover of the jar, the knothole encountered while gouging) add elements of surprise and give the "plot" a twist.

Twice the Carpenter empties the plane of wood shavings, his hands and arms miming their removal, and showing their curling, unfurling lines of force through space. The first time the long, fat wood shavings curve voluminously. The second time, the long delicate wood shavings create a mimetic correspondence in the worker's body. Then, in a surprising sequence of inclinations and rotations of the whole body, the body describing conical movements, the Carpenter – holding the plane in his left hand – maneuvers around the work bench and caresses the wood with his free hand to ascertain if he has accomplished his work well.

3 The compass

Decroux's metal compass, not one for drawing, but one for engraving, has two sharp points which carve into the surface of the wood. The Carpenter finds the compass on his work bench – his body twisting into triple designs, the arm and bust alternating causalities. With a bit of juggling he throws the compass into the air and catches it, and then opens it. (Decroux often observed juggling movements in the way workmen handled their tools, or bar men mixed drinks.) An old tool, and perhaps a bit rusty, the compass resists the Carpenter's efforts to open it, this resistance adding to the drama of the piece. The Carpenter implants the two points into the surface of the plank, and proceeds to turn the compass to inscribe a circle, the body making appropriate compensatory movements. When he finishes the work, the Carpenter closes the compass, again juggles to change it from two hands to one, and replaces it on the surface of the work table.

The real interest of this section, the composition of half-circles, involves turning the head (in triple design) against bust (usually in opposing triple designs), hands and arms working in complex causalities between themselves and with the bust, and the interplay of fixed and moving points. The machine-like precision with which the Carpenter works in this section contrasts with other poetic sections or transitions that show his fatigue, his joy, or his reverie.

4 The jar and screwdriver

Above the Carpenter's work table, a shelf supports a glass jar with a metal top. The Carpenter reaches up for it, removes it from the shelf, lowers it to the center of his body (where most work activity occurs, as Decroux said, as if we had only one arm and hand, coming from the body's center). Then the Carpenter unscrews the jar lid, (with some difficulty, as it is stuck) and places the lid on the shelf. This little sticking moment forces the Carpenter to change his dynamo-rhythm.

He looks for, and, after several seconds of suspense, finds just the right-sized metal screw, which he carefully extracts from the jar, replacing the jar on the wooden shelf. He picks up a small hammer, and with one deft blow, lightly plants the screw vertically into the plank. Then, by lightly caressing the table top (employing one of Decroux's oft-quoted maxims "Do without looking, look without doing") he searches for and eventually finds the screwdriver, which he lines up with the groove in the metal screw head. After several effortful turns, the work becomes easier. At this moment, the Carpenter imagines he hears the Washerwoman calling from the house (he is in the workshop); one hand holds the screwdriver vertical as he turns the body away from that fixed point, and, when he realizes that he has been mistaken, he returns to the last turn of the screwdriver. He then replaces the screwdriver in the box, and in the ensuing chain of causalities he bridges into the next section with the pencil. (These few words describe what happens and a bit more of how; but the complex and unexpected trajectory, speed, and weight render the "what" musical, poetic, and perhaps cubistically shattered, and hence for the most part unidentifiable.)

5 The pencil

Now the Carpenter tentatively searches in his hair for a pencil, finding it behind his right ear. He removes the pencil and his whole body rocks side to side, like a cardboard cut-out structure designed especially to hold a pencil. When the rocking stops, he lowers the pencil along the central axis of the body, and his right hand traces a figure eight with it as the body responds in triple designs (Plate 3.3). To finish the design, the Carpenter pulls the pencil in a straight line, the body lunging to stage left, the left hand and arm acting as a kind of barometer which describes the pressure of the work of the right hand and arm.

6 The gouge

In a funny little cubistic dance, the Carpenter takes from the shelf above the work table – a rectangular wooden box, moves it away from the table, and then back. This movement serves no purpose except as an exploration of the possibilities of side to side movement, the body maintaining its shape, moving in advance of or slower than the box, which the Carpenter pulls along, exaggerating its weight to give it the importance of a significant "dancing partner." After reaching his hands into the box three times to search for the appropriate gouge (the Carpenter's arms respond to the sharpness of the tools with "snail antennae" shock-resonance), he selects a tool, grasping it by its wooden handle. During rehearsals I remember a surprising moment when I grasped the gouge in the box in front of me. Decroux thundered "What are you doing?" I replied that I was taking the gouge. He demanded why I was taking it from the box, insisting instead that I take it from *outside* the box, an inconvenient stretch away. "We are not slaves of realism!" he shouted. In hindsight I see that this inconvenient and illogical stretch makes a beautifully difficult and daring movement, resulting in an unusual and precariously balanced attitude.

Now a complex series of movements transpires, as the gouge shifts from hand to hand, and the Carpenter tests the sharpness of the blade. The Carpenter, using his whole body for leverage, sculpts the wood horizontally and vertically. At a certain point, he encounters

Plate 3.3 Thomas Leabhart in *The Carpenter*, 1974. Here the Carpenter, in a costume designed by Decroux, draws a figure eight on a piece of wood. Photograph: Andrew Kilgore

another knothole (remember the one encountered in planing) against which his gouge rebounds. In a grand gesture of conclusion, he inserts his gouge into the wood just below the knothole, twists the gouge, and expels the knot, which he follows with his eyes, turning his head.

7 Wiping the sweat from his brow: reverie

At the end of the piece, the Carpenter wipes the sweat from his brow, and caresses (again, doing without looking) the plank to test the quality of his work. This moment Decroux described as one of "retrospective reflection." The worker asks himself if he has done well that which he set out to do. In this moment of fatigue, which shows the nobility of manual labor, the Carpenter's intrinsically poetic nature appears. He has fought a Promethean fight against weight, resistance, and inertia, and has won, at least for today. Tomorrow he must begin again.

Even in this cursory description of the "what" and the "how" we encounter necessarily Decroux's convictions and tastes:

1   The "how" is more important than the "what."
2   Manual labor is noble and ennobling.
3   The Carpenter is a poet, but one standing up and working in three dimensions, rather than a seated writer.
4   Counterweights mean something more than lifting weights, but they must first do that accurately.
5   The abstract is the flower of the concrete.

THE WASHERWOMAN

Decroux first created *The Washing* in 1931; he did not call it *The Washerwoman* until 1973, when he added a woman's mask, and a costume that included a little skirt, a kerchief over the head, and a padded bodice (Plate 3.4).

THE WASHERWOMAN: THE "WHAT"

1   Beginning. Testing the water. The Washerwoman begins by standing at the stage center. In an opening protocol, she begins by testing the temperature of the water by touching it lightly with the fingers of both hands.
2   Defining the washtub and washboard.
3   Lifting the bed sheet and placing it on to the washboard.
4   Grasping the soap and projecting it onto the sheet on the washboard. Soaping the sheet, and placing the soap back on the table.
5   Washing the sheet.
6   Scraping the sheet from the washboard, wringing it out, and placing it into a basket.
7   Emptying water from the tub.
8   Transition to stage right, and pumping fresh water into the tub.
9   Transition back to stage left, picking up the basket, and placing the sheet into the water.
10   Transition back to stage right. Rinsing the sheet.
11   Wringing out the sheet and projecting it on a clothes line.
12   Transition to upstage left to find a dry sheet. Transition to downstage center for the ironing.

Plate 3.4 Thomas Leabhart in *The Washerwoman*, 1976. Decroux changed the name of the piece from *The Washing* to *The Washerwoman* in 1973 when he added this all-white costume – hood, mask, gloves, and dress. Photograph: Beatrice Helg

13 Ironing and folding the sheet.
14 Darning a hole in the sheet. Moment of retrospection.
15 Exit drawn up to heaven.

THE WASHERWOMAN: THE "HOW"

1 Beginning

Unlike the Carpenter, the Washerwoman begins at the stage center, facing the audience. Her first movements, which are completely abstract, seem designed to get the body moving gradually, and not to have a basis in the concrete world. Decroux called it simply an "opening protocol." In this sequence of movements, the Washerwoman first inclines the bust to the right, a movement which un-sticks the arms from their position along the sides of the body. The arms, responding to this un-sticking movement, curve into parenthesis shapes, the finger tips sliding up the sides of the legs. The arms then, abruptly moved by the bust snapping back into vertical position, project the arms on to the House Top (one of three possible levels for the arms: the V, the Water Level, and the House Top). The forearms then drop, elbows remaining fixed. The hands then become the motor, flinging themselves downward; when they hit their nadir, they rebound upward, pulling the arms with them, and finally pulling the bust as well into a right inclination with the hands together over the head. These abstract gestures now end, as the hands begin a trajectory downward, toward the tub of water, in order to test the water temperature. The two hands in palette position, one in front of the other, lower slowly toward the water. When the fingers touch and pull backwards suddenly and sharply (a snail antennae causality, indicating that the water is hot) they separate, and when the Washerwoman flings the water droplets from her fingertips the arms fling upward. Again, they pass through some abstract (but very specifically designed) forms before lowering.

This whole sequence is a series of causalities, the arms provoking the bust, the bust provoking the arms, the hands joining in this ballet of cause-and-effect, each movement varying dynamo-rhythm.

Considering it like a ballet or a wrestling match could help us imagine the movement. Instead of a stage full of dancers or a ring full of wrestlers, however, each body part becomes a separate dancer or fighter, provoking the movement of another by pushing or pulling, by slapping or responding to a blow.

2 The washtub and the washboard

The hands lower and discover the wooden tub. The Washerwoman places her thumbs inside the tub and her hands outside. She traces the interior of the tub twice, her thumbs sticking on calcium deposits situated around the water line inside the tub, but only on the half of the circle nearest her body. After finishing the two circles around the tub's interior with her thumbs, she places her fingers and thumbs inside the tub and repeats the two-part circling, sticking on the same calcium deposits. Quick, small vibrations of the actor's biceps create this illusion of sticking on a rough surface. (These same vibratos can project the arm into space, or, when the vibrato occurs in the buttock, can displace the leg.) Then her hands come to rest on the washboard, which she caresses using the same rhythm.

She now confirms the presence of the washboard, continuing the same rhythmic phrase. The small vibrations, which had indicated the calcium deposits along the inside of the tub's rim, now echo the small grooves in the washboard.

3 Lifting the sheet and placing it on the washboard

The Washerwoman has done all her work up to this point in first position. Now, in a surprising moment she leans quickly from side to side, into second position with bent knees. Her body opens from side to side like a compass might open, the legs sticking into the floor like the compass points. She now begins using a counterweight known as "the wool-carding machine" to lift the heavy sheet into the air prior to projecting it onto the washboard. The movement repeats on the left and on the right, on the right turning itself inside out prior to the Washerwoman's jumping into the air to project the sheet, from over the right shoulder, onto the washboard. For this counterweight, she uses "jumping for falling on the head" in triple design (right/right/back changing to left/left/forward). After she places the sheet on the washboard, she gives it two taps which provide a coda to the rhythmic phrase created by lifting and projecting. This sequence demonstrates

Decroux combining two complex counterweights, in triple design, inside a tight rhythmic phrase.

4 The soap

The soap, a large square of *savon de Marseilles*, rests on a low table, stage right of the tub. Using a combination of "doing away with the support" in the lower half of the body, and a large arm circle which provokes a right/right/forward bust design in the upper body, the Washerwoman leans over the soap. Her whole body mirrors the shape of her hand cupped around the soap. Then, as she tightens the body to mime the tightening of her hand around the soap, in an attempt to move the soap, she pulls the upper body toward stage left; the plumb line, which had cut the right ankle, now moves toward the left – the soap, however, remains firmly stuck to the table. This movement perfectly reflects Decroux's counterweight theories: the soap itself has almost no weight, and the Washerwoman can, in reality, move it easily without counterweights. However, this kind of movement – banal and without "drama" – Decroux preferred to heighten or amplify with the use of counterweights, imagining the soap much heavier, and the Washerwoman much weaker, in order to dramatize the conflict between the two.

With a second effort – pulling again toward stage left, the soap un-sticks and the Washerwoman's body changes from a curve left (left/left forward bust design) to a high right/right/forward bust design and the body in a curve with the chord of the arc inclined to stage left. Here the Washerwoman, unable to project the soap without this help, thrusts her right hip against her right elbow, projecting the soap – still in her hand – on a long diagonal upward. Moving in opposition to the body, the soap changes direction at the top of its trajectory, and the Washerwoman brings it back down to the washboard, her body again finding balance on two feet, facing front.

The Washerwoman now soaps the sheet.

All these maneuvers with the soap (including putting it back on the table, an equally complex composition, which I will not describe) Decroux uses to explore the idea of lines of force. Lines of force, he explained, are the trajectories people, objects and events would take if not limited by lack of strength or social pressures. For example, any simple event, like yawning, or putting on a jacket, could take place in a restricted space (an elevator) or in an unrestricted space (a large garden).

The performer's desire to remain inconspicuous and discreet or, in the absence of spectators, the performer's lack of inhibition, would limit or free the movements. In following a line of force, allowing the gesture to attain fullness unknown in polite society, Decroux said we did not lie, but instead revealed a deeper (nonrealistic) truth that oftentimes remains unexpressed.

5 Washing the sheet

The Washerwoman now inclines her entire body (Eiffel Tower) from left to right, propelling her hand across the sheet on the washboard. As she continues her work, her movements become smaller and faster, finishing with quick, staccato movements of the bust instigated by her seeing a spot she would like to remove from the sheet. In the midst of these fast, short movements, a curious thing happens. The Washerwoman thinks she hears the Carpenter calling her, and she leans back in a spiral around to her right, in a pattern similar to the one made by her husband, the Carpenter, when he thinks he hears her calling him. This moment of "intertextuality" finished (she was mistaken; he had not called), she completes the sequence by removing the spot with short quick movements, returning then to her Eiffel Tower inclination to the left.

6 Scraping the sheet from the washboard

The Washerwoman now scrapes the sheet from the washboard (using a hand design, appropriate for the maneuver: the Salamander) wrings it out, and throws into a wicker basket. The whole body participates in the wringing; as the body closes in upon itself, it becomes a small, compacted sphere which squeezes out the last drops of moisture. Again the Washerwoman uses her hips to project this compacted sheet into the basket. As the hips initiate the movement, the arms and the rest of the body follow. This tying and untying, tightening and loosening of the sheet and the body, creates a strikingly curvilinear design, beautiful in its truthfulness to the action portrayed.

7 Emptying out the tub

The Washerwoman's previous gestures have propelled her to stage left. She now turns abruptly into profile, facing stage right. In one of the most spectacular counterweights of the piece, she drops down and places both hands under the bottom of the very heavy wooden tub filled with water. She then lifts the tub far enough above the earth in order for her to change her grip, from a symmetrical to an asymmetrical one, and again uses her pelvis, this time as a prop for her left elbow, to continue raising the tub. She succeeds in upending the tub and completely emptying out the water. The tub has become progressively lighter during the lifting process, as water has been spilling out of it. Now, completely empty, it becomes almost a toy (albeit a still comparatively heavy one); the last moments of pouring out water are accomplished in an arabesque *penché*, the supporting foot momentarily in *relevé*. As the Washerwoman subsequently drops the tub heavily to the ground, she scoops her body quickly backward, arms flying up, to escape it as it falls.

8 Transition to stage right and pumping fresh water into the tub

The Washerwoman now moves from stage left to stage right in a semicircular pattern around the washtub. Her body reflects the shape of the tub she circles. Her feet slide in small, staccato movements, one heel knocking into the other in order to advance. She arrives on the other side of the tub, takes the pump handle in her hand and begins to lift and lower it. This counterweight allows for the initial movements required to unstick the pump; her first movements reflect the dry gasps the pumping makes until water eventually rises in the pipe and the subsequent movements flow more graciously. Once the tub has filled with water, she pushes the pump handle completely down, expelling the last drop of water from the pipe, as her rising left arm and hand imitate the water flowing from the spout.

9 Transition back to stage left, picking up the basket, and placing the sheet in the clear water

The Washerwoman, after retracing the half-circle around the washtub and arriving stage left, engages in a precarious Luxury Balance (this term from Barba's Theatre Anthropology describes perfectly the arabesque she performs as she tips further and further forward on to the bent front leg) to grasp and lift the basket from the floor to a braced position against her body. Here the logic of the composition breaks down somewhat: the Washerwoman removes several clumps of laundry from the basket even though she placed only one clump – the tightly wrung sheet – into it. It is doubtless that this repetition adds rhythmic interest to the sequence. The whole upper body – head, neck, and chest – work together with the right arm and hand to form a large mechanical crane-like structure to close around the compacted spheres of wet cloth, to lift them, transport them, and drop them into the clear water. The contracting of the upper body and right arm occurs against the immobile left arm and hand, holding the wicker basket balanced upon the left hip. She then takes the handle of the basket, which has been braced against her left pelvis, into her right hand, and again passing through a precarious Luxury Balance, lowers the now empty basket to the ground.

10 Transition back to stage right and rinsing the clothes

Before she has completed the movement of placing the basket on the floor, she has turned her body inside out and now faces the opposite direction, in the shape we now recognize as the one which will take her around the half-circle previously described – the upstage side of the curved washtub (see entry 8). Once there, she jumps – with a small, percussive step – sharply into a profile position to the audience and begins to rinse the sheet in the clear water. After rinsing several times with two hands, using a backward inclination of the half-Eiffel as a counterweight, the sheet becomes more fluid in the water, and she shifts the sheet to one hand. Here an undulatory movement beginning with an alternation of tension and relaxation in the actor's right bicep creates the illusion that the sheet is unfurling into the water. Then the actor, with the right hand, pulls the sheet through a trough created by the left.

11 Wringing out the sheet and placing it on the clothes line

She then begins to wring the sheet, and passes through a series of movements which often provoke laughter. Here the wet and flexible sheet for a few brief seconds becomes a rifle and the Washerwoman becomes a soldier standing at attention, performing choreographed maneuvers with the rifle. Then, just as quickly as the "rifle" appeared, it disappears and becomes again a tightly wound, yet still flexible, sheet. Next the Washerwoman opens the sheet and through an unexpected series of movements parallel to the audience and parallel to a clothes-line which "appears" along the proscenium line, she projects the wet sheet on to the line and affixes it with clothespins.

12 Transition to upstage left to find a dry sheet

Now we must imagine that a second sheet, which she had earlier stretched out on a different line upstage, has dried. The Washerwoman's movements become billowy, like a dry sheet on a warm breezy day. She turns upstage and there embraces a dried sheet, takes the clothespins from it, and, turning downstage, throws it forward (Plate 3.5), allowing the air to catch under the sheet, and finally stretches it out on an ironing board.

13 Ironing and folding the sheets

The Washerwoman uses an old-fashioned cast-iron iron which was heated on a coal stove. She lifts the iron and approaches it carefully toward the side of her face, testing the warmth by making a translation of the head toward the iron, and quickly pulling her cheek away as she confirms the temperature. (This movement Decroux described as the snail antennae, because of its slow approach and sudden recoil.) Then the whole body engages in the counterweight of ironing. The body itself becomes a large iron, and the pushing through the body serves as the pressure which, combined with heat, removes the wrinkles from the sheet. She irons first in one direction, then in another; between heavy, angular sequences of ironing, she lightly folds the sheet first one way, then another, scooping out the body to make room for the circular motion of the hand and sheet. She finally pulls it from the table, as the whole body glides backward with smooth, practiced efficiency.

14 Darning a hole in the sheet – moment of retrospection

Now a darning egg – an egg-shaped wooden support for cloth used while darning – appears in one hand, as does a darning needle and

Plate 3.5 Corinne Soum in *The Washerwoman*, 1994. Soum, who studied with Decroux from 1978 to 1984, also served as his teaching assistant. With Steven Wasson, she directs the Théâtre de l'Ange Fou and a corporeal mime school in London. Photograph: Lionel Forneaux

thread in the other. The Washerwoman begins to darn the sheet. Never mind that it has been neatly folded on the table. Without reopening the sheet, she begins to work, first in one direction, and then at right angles to the first direction, in order to reweave the fabric of the sheet. After four such cross-hatchings, (performed to the rhythm of a section of *Swan Lake* playing in the actor's mind but, of course, not heard – only seen – by the audience), the Washerwoman makes a step upstage (while still facing the audience) and begins a fifth stitch. This stitch, however, becomes much larger, the thread much longer, and carries the Washerwoman into designs of the body which fully explore the lines of force which had remained latent in the first four stitches. Decroux said that in realistic theatre, the longer one sews the shorter the thread gets, while in his theatre the reverse can happen. At the end of the fifth stitch, the Washerwoman replaces the darning needle in the lapel of her apron, and looks retrospectively over her morning's work.

15 Exit and "ascending"

As she (still rather hesitatingly) walks on a long diagonal upstage left, the Washerwoman pauses, her body balloons upward, and seems to ascend into the clouds, having fully and beautifully accomplished her work.

Plate 3.6(a)–(d) shows Marise Flash in *The Washing*.

SUMMARY

These two works, certainly among the most unusual theatre pieces of the twentieth century, attempt to redefine theatre practice, as well as to implement a new art form: Corporeal Mime. They exist without written text, and in their first productions, were entirely produced by the actor-creator, Decroux himself. In subsequent productions, Decroux as director taught the movements he had created for himself to successive generations of actors. The weighted, purposeful movements of these pieces clearly represent a vocabulary derived from work rather than dance. Video documentation exists of Steven Wasson, Corinne Soum, and Thomas Leabhart performing these works.

Decroux added Bach's Brandenburg Concerto No. 5 in B Major as a support for *The Carpenter*, and Ravel's *Bolero* for *The Washerwoman*. In both cases, the musical composition lasts longer than the performance,

Plate 3.6(a)–(d) Marise Flash in *The Washing*, 2006. Flash, who worked with Decroux from 1949–55, has taught movement for actors, mime and improvisation, at the Piccolo Teatro in Milan since 1954. Photograph: Mila Casali

Plate 3.6(a)–(d) Continued

Plate 3.6(a)–(d) Continued

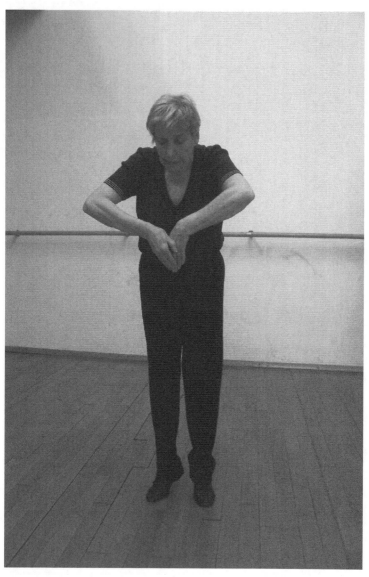

Plate 3.6(a)–(d) Continued

he simply faded the music at the end of each. He insisted on what he called a "music of repetition" – a music which had a clearly defined rhythm (clearly audible in each of these compositions). Contrasting to the regular rhythm of these musical compositions, Decroux wanted the actor himself to embody the irregular rhythm – pause, weight, resistance, hesitation, and surprise – reflecting the movement of thought and work.

In a filming in 1973, Decroux added white mask, hood, body suit and gloves to completely conceal the actor, making him an archetype in both compositions – a kind of marionette figure. This costume for *The Washerwoman* included a head scarf, padded bodice, short white skirt, and a woman's mask.

These two pieces represent only part of Decroux's impressive accomplishment of almost one hundred works, and while they are typical of his approach, one cannot easily describe his creative work which included many and varied approaches. Comedy's notable absence from Decroux's work reflected his belief that an art must first be serious, and only later and secondarily permit itself to entertain. His *Mischevious Spirit* comes closest to comedy, in whose creation Maximilian Decroux claims a strong hand, affirming that his father had no talent for staging comedy (Decroux 2001: 79).

CORPOREAL MIME TECHNIQUE

Practical exercises with immediate applications

After examining the first three chapters of this book, the reader will understand the impossibility of learning Corporeal Mime without a qualified teacher and years of daily lessons. Even with the detailed written instructions and drawings in this chapter, you will find it impossible to approximate Corporeal Mime's "music" – a rhythm of cause and effect, of shock and resonance, a lively vibrato – which one cannot communicate except in person. Despite Decroux's proficiency in writing and speaking, his creation, Corporeal Mime, like Chinese opera, bio-mechanics, and the Noh play, remains a detailed and specific kinesthetic art. Decroux often joked that Corporeal Mime was "easy to do poorly."

I have, however, extrapolated from each exercise some suggested **immediate applications**. Decroux's études are psychophysical, the physical taking precedence over the psychological (or *imaginative*, a word he would have preferred) in the first learning years, and the imaginative taking precedence only after one has thoroughly assimilated the foundation. The uninitiated often mistakenly think that the physical suffices when, in fact, it merely opens the door to Decroux's theatre of imagery. These **immediate applications** try to bridge this gap for the student reader, connecting the two worlds – the physical and the imaginative.

Plate 4.1 Etienne Decroux and Thomas Leabhart in the basement school in Boulogne-Billancourt, 1970. The window to the right opens out to the garden; white curtains close across the end of the room to create a more theatrical space for improvisations. Unattributed photograph

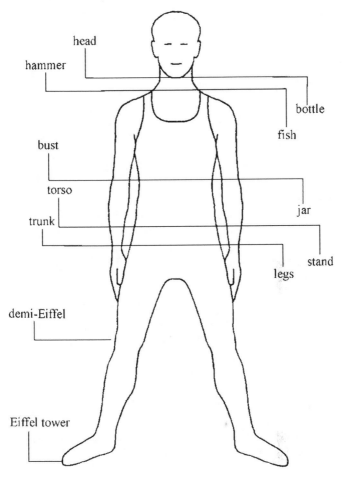

Figure 4.1 Decroux articulates the human body

The following exercises represent different areas of Decroux's work while sharing his basic premise that the body must become articulated like a keyboard. Before we learn to play the scales, let us learn the names of the various keys or parts (Figure 4.1). While one may incline, rotate, or translate any of these parts, one usually first learns inclinations on the lateral plane.

INCLINATIONS ON A LATERAL PLANE

1 Lateral scale

Incline the head, and return; incline the Hammer (head plus neck in a straight line), then return; incline the Bust (head plus neck plus chest in a straight line), then return; incline the Torso (head plus neck plus chest plus waist in a straight line), then return; incline the trunk from a conform axle (head plus neck plus chest plus waist plus pelvis, in a straight line, moving around an absolutely fixed point found on the same side of the pelvis toward which one inclines), then return; incline the trunk from a contrary axle (the same except you move around a different absolutely fixed point, the one on the side of the pelvis *opposite* to the direction to which you incline), then return; incline the trunk from a central axle (the same except you move around a relatively fixed point, about one inch below the navel, that is, you raise up on that point on the central line, and then incline), then return; incline the Eiffel Tower (the whole body inclines in a straight line from the fixed point of the foot), then return. See Figures 4.2–4.9.

After learning this exercise to the side, you may perform it forward, backward, in rotation, in rotation on an inclined plane, or in double or triple designs (see p. 20 for explanation of triple designs).

One may perform these segmented movements quickly, attacking each movement vigorously, or in uniformly slow motion, or with any other combination of dynamo-rhythm. One must, however, regardless of the dynamo-rhythm, achieve clear separations between and among the parts. Decroux often said that immobility was an action – you must work just as hard to keep the part which should not move from doing so as you work to move the part which you want to move.

Decroux insisted that the actor perform even this seemingly dull, dry technical exercise with verve, élan, a brightness in the eye – anything to prevent it from looking formulaic. He never wanted the actor to become an empty robot, and if actors performing Corporeal Mime sometimes look this way, they are probably still struggling to remember the next movement phrase, or to keep from falling.

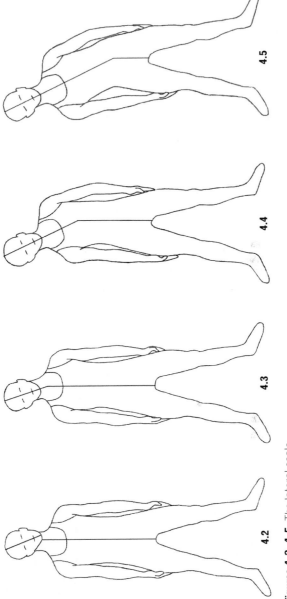

Figures 4.2–4.5 The lateral scale

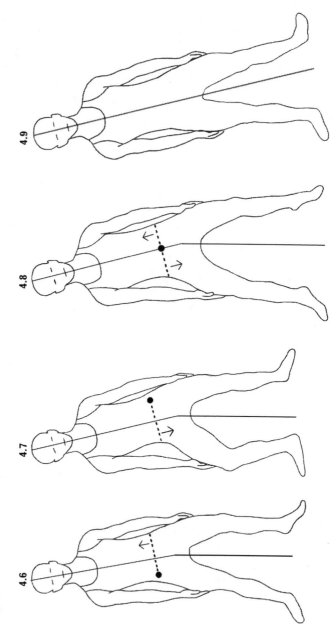

Figures 4.6–4.9 The lateral scale

Immediate application

If you are working on a scene or a monologue, at certain appropriate moments incline, translate, or rotate just the head, the bust, or the trunk, while keeping the rest of the body still. This gives focus to your acting, maintaining an inner energy which escapes only in selected and controlled movements and speech. "Clean" acting projects at greater distances, and makes a greater impact. However, if you perform these inclinations, rotations, and translations (Figures 4.10–4.12) in a mechanical way, or at an inappropriate time, the results become stilted and unintentionally comic. (Read Henri Bergson's *On Laughter*.) An actor who maintains stillness, except when intentionally moving, always attracts attention, while actors who shuffle and fidget quickly tire us.

Figure 4.10 Head inclination

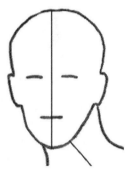

Figure 4.11 Head translation

Figure 4.12 Head rotation

CONTRADICTIONS ON A LATERAL PLANE

Incline the head to the right, and the bottle to the left, then return to center; incline the hammer to the right, and the fish to the left, then return to center; incline the bust to the right, the vase to the left, return to center; incline the torso to the right, the stand to the left, then return; incline the trunk to the right, the legs to the left, then return. See Figures 4.13–4.19.

Immediate application

Physical and emotional contradictions lie at the heart of the drama that Corporeal Mime embodies. As Decroux said, a man on a ship leaving New York harbor for France looks back wistfully toward the Statue of Liberty as the ship moves inexorably toward Europe. Find appropriate moments in the monologue or scene you are currently working on to let the body show contradictions inherent in the situation – for example, the bust (the heart) moving in one direction while the head (intelligence) moves in another, or the pelvis (procreative and digestive elements) pulling the rest of the body in one direction, while the head or heart pull it in the other. (Read Ted Shawn's book on François Delsarte, *Every Little Movement*.)

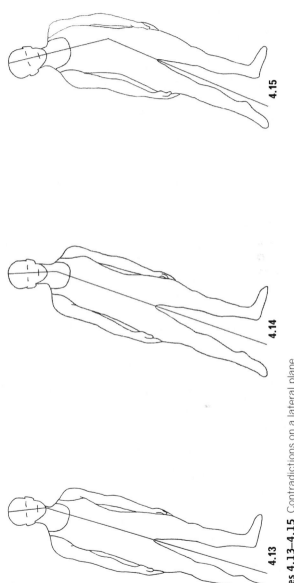

Figures 4.13–4.15 Contradictions on a lateral plane

Figures 4.16–4.19 Contradictions on a lateral plane

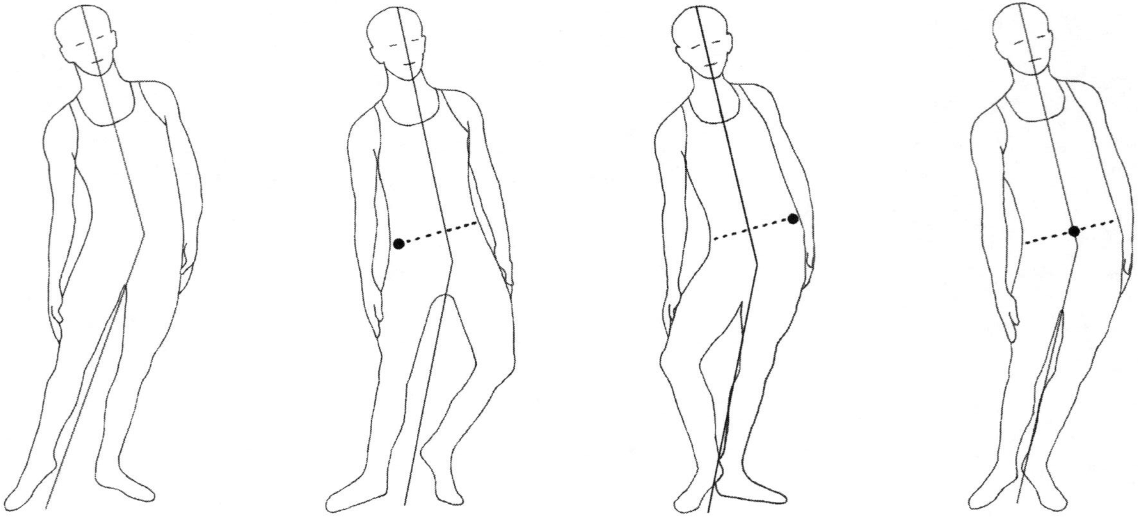

SEGMENTED MOVEMENT, LATERAL SCALE, CUMULATIVELY CURVED (THE SPINE MOVING LIKE A CHAIN)

Instead of forming a bar (as in exercises 1 and 2) with segmented movements, one may form a curved line or chain: head (this is the first movement of the bar scale and the chain scale); head plus neck (curving rather than re-established on the oblique); and so on (always keeping a high curve of all the links in the chain) until the whole body becomes engaged, shifting the weight on to one leg. See Figure 4.20.

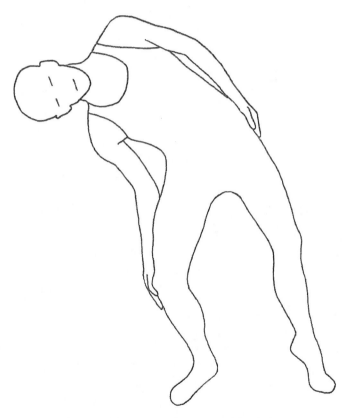

Figure 4.20 Segmented curve on a lateral plane

Immediate application

In moments of reflection or reverie, the head, neck, and bust incline to the side. The actor may arrive at these places all at once (if appropriate), or one element at a time, the head beginning the movement which pulls the neck and chest, or the bottommost element pulling the upper ones digressively. Find an appropriate moment in your monologue or scene where this might occur. In a nonrealistic play or situation, one could continue the segmented movement to the end, including the legs. Of course, the movements will look more "behavioral" and "organic" if performed in three dimensions rather than to the side exclusively. If your attempts appear inappropriate and ridiculous, you must experiment until you find the appropriate moment for the appropriate movement. Do not forget to try "reductions" of large movements, reducing the movement to a size appropriate to the style of your scene or monologue.

One may return to the vertical digressively, beginning with the legs, or progressively, beginning with the head, going to the opposite curve.

PULLING AN EXTENSOR

Again, the goal of this exercise is not for a spectator to recognize the action; in it the actor reduces pulling to its essence – a study of the counterweight Decroux called the wool carding machine (see p. 80).

The activity dissected below consists of taking the handle of a body-building device, an extensor, and, holding the handle, pulling its springs into an extreme diagonal, and then releasing it, the springs returning it to their original position.

The actor begins on the same diagonal as above, again in second position. His left foot pushes the Eiffel Tower to the right, and a right/right/back of the bust unfurls the arms. The right arm moves across the body as the chest assumes a left/right/back design. See Figures 4.21–4.25.

The hand, one finger at a time, grips the handle.

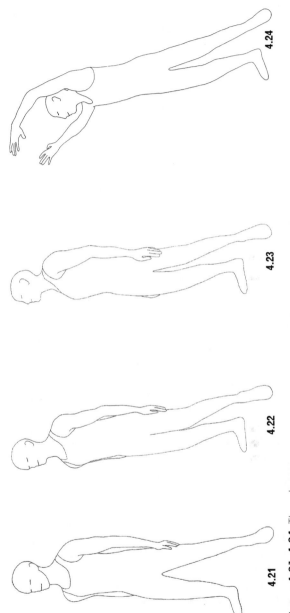

4.21

4.22

4.23

4.24

Figures 4.21–4.24 The extensor

After three small preparatory breaths of the body (raising and lowering from the feet), the chest moves from left/right/back to left/left/forward, straightening the arm; the right knee bends, moving the right foot into a place occupied by the left foot; the left knee straightens and moves the left foot out of the way of the right foot. One should eventually perform these three separate movements together, creating a cubistic pulling movement, which brings the wrist of the right hand to a resting position against the left crest of the ilium. See Figures 4.26–4.28.

Decroux's premise remains that the arm and hand can do nothing of themselves; they must seek help from the body. Now the body, propelled by the left foot, helps the actor to pull the handle upward, but always in full contact with the body (one is always stronger in a spherical shape, he often said – if the arms separate themselves too far from the body, he cautioned, they lose their strength).

The wrist traces a line from the ilium to the center of the body, across the sternum (between the pectorals or breasts) and on to the top of the sternum. Now the foot performs a movement known in Corporeal Mime as a "cannon," the left foot pushing into the ground and propelling the body toward the right. The chest design changes to right/right/back, the plumb line dropped from the center of the body cuts the right ankle. See Figure 4.29.

As the actor, with his weight now well behind and under the right hand and arm, pushes the right hand slowly toward the upstage right corner, he performs a second "cannon" (a rebounding – like the ricochet of a firing cannon) from the left foot with the feet and legs on to the right foot, thereby increasing his strength enough to straighten the right arm entirely. See Figures 4.30 and 4.31.

Now, the return. The body leans away from the straightened arm, which lowers; then the arm bends as the hand approaches the chest. The wrist bends and the knuckles knock against the right pectoral. As the body turns left into a c-curve, the left fist traces an "eyebrow" above the right pectoral. See Figures 4.32 and 4.33. As the c-curve inclines backward, the left fist retraces the "eyebrow" forward, and as the chord of the arc inclines backward, the flexed wrist descends between the pectorals. See Figure 4.34.

As the wool-carding machine digs into the earth, the c-curve inclining backward, the arm raises and lowers along the median line of the body, and as it leaves the body, the c-curve begins to reverse itself, the c occupying

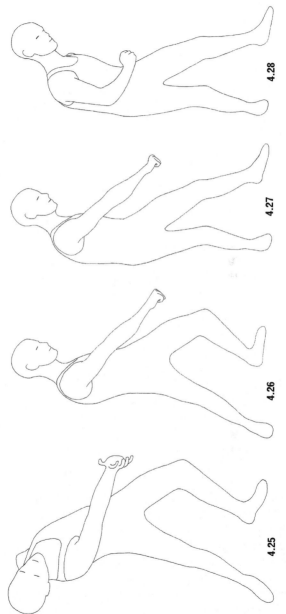

4.25 **4.26** **4.27** **4.28**

Figures 4.25–4.28 The extensor

Figures 4.29–4.32 The extensor

4.29   4.30    4.31    4.32

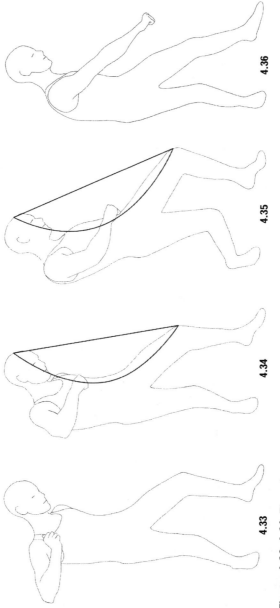

Figures 4.33–4.36 The extensor

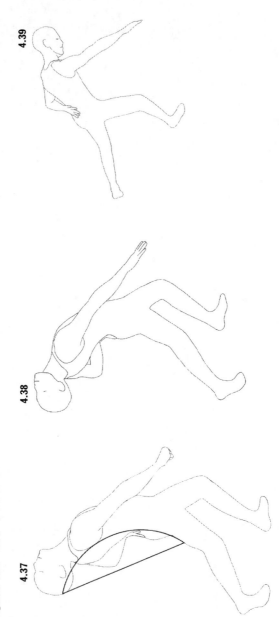

Figures 4.37–4.39 The extensor

4.37

4.38

4.39

the back rather than the front of the body. See Figures 4.35, 4.36, and 4.37. When the arm extends fully forward toward the lower stage left diagonal, the hand releases and the force pulls the body forward – Figures 4.38 and 4.39.

An almost limitless number of possible extensor origins and destinations exist: imagine standing inside a cube. The actor can take a handle from any corner of the cube and extend the springs toward the opposite corner. Or the actor can take the handle from the middle of any surface of the cube – the four sides, and the top and the bottom – and pull the springs toward the middle of the opposite side of the cube.

The extensor exercise divides into two main types: reaching across the body to take the handle, as in the exercise described above, or reaching on to the same side of the body. Reaching below and above the body are variations of the same side reach.

Immediate application

This exercise represents an advanced level of work in Corporeal Mime, yet it contains elements which can apply to more ordinary kinds of drama. The eyes alone could pull someone or something toward us. Try this. The eyes and the head could pull. The eyes, the head, the neck, etc., could pull someone or something toward us. Were this exercise reduced in size but not intensity, without movement of the arms , an actor could use it as a movement score for psychological drama – thus becoming a "metaphysical counter-weight." Try to create a reduced version of the above score. Rehearse it until you know it well. Be sure that the essence of pulling remains. Use this movement score appropriately and behaviorally (in a convincingly natural way) in a scene or a monologue.

Most drama pushes or pulls physical or psychological weight. Imagine a moment in your current monologue or scene work where you might push against a scene partner or an idea. How would the whole body, especially the point three inches below the navel, become involved in this activity? What dynamics come into play? You may push with just the eyes, or just the head and the eyes, or just the head, chest, waist, and eyes. Adapt this pushing appropriately to the circumstances of your scene or monologue, using the parts of the body, and the intensity, appropriate to the situation.

DOUBLE, TRIPLE, AND QUADRUPLE DESIGNS

Why does one incline a body part?

- To approach someone affectionately or aggressively.
- To think or reflect or to muse.
- To push or to pull.

Why does one rotate a body part?

- To look at someone or something.
- To push or to pull.

Why does one translate a body part?

- To listen (translation of the ear – on the sides of the head – to the side).
- To look (translation of the eyes – in the head – forward).
- To push or to pull.

The Head, the Bust, the Trunk, and the Eiffel Tower can perform double, triple, or quadruple Designs. The four elements available to the actor are:

1 Rotations (usually one-eighth of a circle).
2 Inclinations forward or back.
3 Inclinations right or left.
4 Translations forward and back.

One may invent a large number of combinations of these elements to create communicative dramatic designs.

Immediate application

When the actor has completely assimilated these combinations of movements, one can perform three movements in one. These rotations and inclinations easily lend themselves to any number of images which enrich their playing. The actor's imagination supplies different substances through which one moves, or different qualities of light, or even different odors or colors. Decroux never objected when these imaginative elements came secondarily, inspired by the forms. He encouraged us with his own rich poetic metaphors, singing, and storytelling, to go beyond a mere reproduction of the shell of the exercise.

Visit a museum which has a collection of classical sculpture, or obtain a book of photographs of Greek or Roman statues, or the work of Rodin. Observe the works closely and try to recreate one or two of them in your body. Note the rotations and inclinations of the head, bust, and trunk. Learn a "score" of five or six statues which you can perform without thinking. Use these in your scene or monologue. If you use them inappropriately, they will become ridiculous; reduce the degree of inclination and rotation until the stature becomes behavioral, organic, and appropriate to your scene or monologue.

STAGES OF CONSCIOUSNESS

1   Begin sitting on the front edge of a chair, one foot under the chair, one foot in front. The back, rounded in relaxation, should not touch the chair back. The head, inclined to the left side, places the face parallel to the audience. This stage is called sleeping with the eyes closed.

2   As the eyelids flutter, the head slowly moves toward the vertical (be careful not to move any other part of the body).

3   The eyelids open widely, revealing completely relaxed, asymmetrical, and out-of-focus eyes. This stage is called sleeping with the eyes open.

4   The eyes come into clear focus, while the face remains completely relaxed, mouth slightly open. This is called seeing and not understanding.

5   The head then lifts upward, pulling the neck and the remainder of the relaxed spine to a standing vertical. The mouth closes, and the face and scalp tighten. This stage is called seeing and understanding.

6   The body lifts off the chair, and the person becomes completely vertical standing up. Here one must exercise caution not to allow

the pelvis to fall into an anterior tilt as one stands, creating a "wobble" through the spine.

7   One takes three steps forward, ending in second position. This is called seeing and understanding and acting upon what one understands.

8   Now we fall slowly, going through the above phases, as the spine crumples and the body rolls on the ground.

Immediate application

Every character in dramatic literature occupies one of these stages of consciousness, and during the play he or she moves upward or downward on the scale. Try to identify the character you are currently working on in terms of this scale of consciousness.

MOVEMENT RESEARCH: HOW TO CREATE A "MOVEMENT SCORE"

In my early days of teaching, I devised an exercise that permitted even beginning students to create a movement score that they could interpret and perform. Although Decroux did not create this exercise, it comes directly from his teaching, especially our improvisation with objects. Decroux describes work with the prop this way:

The manipulation of properties and the act of going toward them or leaning over them should, instead of interrupting the action's affective current, provide it with a further opportunity, and the best, to take place. Feeling is better demonstrated when applied to a concrete action. Separate from this concrete action, it can become exhibitionistic. The property, like iron, conducts heat.

(Decroux 1985: 125)

In order to begin movement research, choose a quotidian activity like putting on a coat or shirt. Begin by placing the shirt on the back of a chair, and by standing behind the chair facing front. Rehearse putting on the shirt in a naturalistic manner. Count the number of movements. Work carefully to avoid "diphthongs" which occur in real life – for example, reaching for the shirt and grasping it in one movement. In fact, the sequence might look something like this:

1   reach for the shirt;
2   grasp the collar in your hand;
3   lift the shirt from the chair back;
4   etc.

Memorize this sequence of movements. Putting on a shirt, for example, could have between 50 and 60 individual movements, especially when you count the detailed movements of finding each button and buttoning it (three or four movements for each button).

When you perform this "primary text" for your colleagues, it should not look especially theatrical. You should resemble an ordinary person putting on a shirt, but, through force of repetition, and the elimination of "diphthongs," the movements will have taken on a greater clarity, making the sequence appear somewhat like "magic realism."

Now that you have created a "primary text" you may allow it to direct you to create a "secondary text." This secondary text consists of allowing the primary text to create a logical and coherent response in the trunk of the body – in the core – comprising a change of level (in space) and plane (of the body). If you change just one of these elements, your secondary text will appear stilted and decorative. If you change both, logically following the line of force suggested by the primary text, your secondary text will allow the primary one to blossom. Imagine that the primary text is a bud, the secondary text the full blown flower.

Suddenly, your first composition (the primary text) has begun to wrestle with the body; it has pushed and pulled the body into an extraordinary and theatrical way of moving, but one which is still honest and authentic vis-à-vis the original task. It may take some weeks of daily rehearsal to establish a coherent and logical secondary text. When you have succeeded, you may begin to phrase this secondary text.

Begin by placing two moments of dynamic immobility. Dynamic immobility is a stillness inside of which the motor continues to turn. A fly buzzing against a window, trying to get out, is one of Decroux's examples for this state.

These moments of immobility divide the composition into three acts. Now begin to phrase each act, varying speed and weight. You will find

Plate 4.2
Madame and Monsieur Decroux in their kitchen in Boulogne-Billancourt, 1975. Decroux, dressed in his usual black boxing shorts and long-sleeved shirt, waits by the door to shake each student's hand at the end of the class. Photograph: Christian Mattis Schmocker

Plate 4.3 Etienne Decroux in his basement studio, 1975. This photograph captures the playful and whimsical aspects of Decroux's personality. Photograph: Christian Mattis Schmocker

that you naturally move at a certain speed, with a certain weight (degree of resistance). Now explore the areas that are unfamiliar to you. Play a series of movements faster or more slowly than is your custom. Find moments of great resistance (imagine trying to unscrew a tightly secured jar lid) which suddenly break (as when the lid comes loose). Find moments which "stutter" or "stammer." Only allow yourself the two moments of immobility. Otherwise you will (naturally) stop after every movement to think of what the next one is, and your composition will remain quite static. You must play it as you would a musical composition, skillfully and even soulfully, but without conscious thought.

You may add verbal text judiciously to this movement score, placing it mostly during your dynamic immobilities, and before and after the task. You may create a reduced version of this activity, without the original object, in which you "subjectify" the movements, making it seem like you are wrestling with your thought and not with an object, rather than making a kind of pantomime without the accessory.

BIBLIOGRAPHY

BOOKS AND ARTICLES

Alaniz, Sirlei (2004) "La Notion de dynamo-rythme chez Etienne Decroux et ses successeurs," Memoire, University of Paris 8.

Barba, Eugenio (1997) "The Hidden Master," *Words on Decroux II*, Claremont, CA: Mime Journal.

Barba, Eugenio, and Savarese, Nicola (eds.) (1991) *A Dictionary of Theatre Anthropology: The Secret Art of the Performer*, trans. Richard Fowler, New York: Routledge.

Barrault, Jean-Louis (1951) *Reflections on the Theatre*, trans. Barbara Wall, London: Rockliff.

—— (1972) *Souvenirs pour demain*, Paris: Seuil.

Barthes, Roland (1977) *Image, Music, Text*, trans. Stephen Heath, New York: Hill and Wang.

—— (1986) *A Barthes Reader*, New York: Hill and Wang.

Benhaïm, Guy (2003) "Etienne Decroux, ou la chronique d'un siècle," *Etienne Decroux, Mime Corporeal*, ed. Patrick Pezin, Saint-Jean-de-Védas: L'Entretemps édition.

Bentley, Eric (1953) "The Purism of Etienne Decroux," *In Search of Theatre*, New York: Alfred A. Knopf.

Bogart, Anne (2001) *A Director Prepares*, New York: Routledge.

Cole, David (1977) *The Theatrical Event*, Middletown, CT: Wesleyan University Press.

Copeau, Jacques (1931) *Souvenirs du Vieux Colombier*, Paris: Les Nouvelle Editions Latines.

—— (1990) *Texts on Theatre*, ed. and trans. John Rudlin and Norman H. Paul, New York: Routledge.

—— (2000) *Registres VI: L'Ecole du Vieux Colombier*, Paris: Gallimard.

Craig, Edward Gordon (2001) "At Last a Creator in the Theatre, from the Theatre," *An Etienne Decroux Album*, Claremont, CA: Mime Journal.

Decroux, Etienne (1942) "Copeau ne peut plus maitriser le mime qu'il a dechaine," Unpublished Manuscript, Box 1 (No. 75), Fonds Decroux, Bibliothèque Nationle de France.

—— (1948) "De la personality d'Etienne Decroux," Unpublished Manuscript, Box 2 (No. 76), Fonds Decroux, Bibliothèque Nationale de France.

—— (1950) "Autobiographie d'Etienne Decroux," Unpublished Manuscript, Box 2 (No. 76), Fonds Decroux, Bibliothèque Nationale de France.

—— (1953) "Mai 1953," Unpublished Manuscript, Box 2 (No. 57), Fonds Decroux, Bibliothèque Nationale de France.

—— (1971) inscription dated October 25 in Henri Bergson's *le Rire*.

—— (1972) inscription dated July 16 in *Paroles sur le mime*.

—— (1978) "The Mask," *Etienne Decroux 80th Birthday Issue,* Claremont, CA: Mime Journal.

—— (1985) *Words on Mime*, trans. Mark Piper, Claremont, CA: Mime Journal.

—— (2001) "Insulting the Audience," *An Etienne Decroux Album*, Claremont, CA: Mime Journal.

—— (2003) "L'Interview Imaginaire," *Etienne Decroux, Mime Corporeal*, ed. Patrick Pezin, Saint-Jean-de-Védas: L'Entretemps édition.

Dorcy, Jean (1945) Unidentified newspaper clipping, Fonds Decroux, Bibliotheque Nationale de France.

—— (1961) *The Mime*, New York: Robert Speller and Sons Ltd.

Fogal, Dean (1993) "Etienne Decroux – Outside Paris Proper" *Words on Decroux*, Claremont, CA: Mime Journal.

Grotowski, Jerzy (1997a) "La 'ligne organique' au théâtre et dans le rituel," leçon inaugaurale au Théâtre des Bouffes du Nord–Paris, Vilefranche-du-Perigord: Le livre qui parle, March 24.

—— (1997b) "La 'ligne organique' au théâtre et dans le rituel," au Théâtre de l'Odeon–Paris, Vilefranche-du-Perigord: Le livre qui parle, June 2.

—— (2002) *Towards a Poor Theatre*, ed. Eugenio Barba, New York: Routledge.

Kusler, Barbara Anne (1974) "Jacques Copeau's Theatre School: L'Ecole du Vieux-Colombier, 1920–1929," Diss. University of Wisconsin.

Lalli, Gina (1993) "Amazing Moments with Etienne Decroux," *Words on Decroux*, Claremont, CA: Mime Journal.

Lehmann, Hans-Thies (2006) *Postdramatic Theatre*, New York: Routledge.

Leigh, Barbara Kusler (1979) *Jacques Copeau's School for Actors*, Allendale, MI: Mime Journal.

Lorelle, Yves (1974) *L'Expression Corporelle: du mime sacré au mime de theater*, Paris: la Renaissance du Livre.

Marceau, Marcel (1958) "The Language of the Heart," *Theatre Arts*, March, 58–70.

—— (1991) "Paroles pour un mime," *Telex-Danse No. 38*, June, 12.

Mitchell, W.J.T. (1995) "Representation," *Critical Terms for Literary Study*, eds. Frank Lentricchia and Thomas McLaughlin, Chicago, IL: University of Chicago Press.

Muray, Simon (2003) *Jacques Lecoq*, London: Routledge.

Pinaud, Nicole (2003) "Le Minotaure," *Etienne Decroux, Mime Corporeal*, ed. Patrick Pezin, Saint-Jean-de-Védas: L'Entretemps édition.

Pronko, Leonard (1967) *Theatre East and West, Perspectives Toward a Total Theatre*, Berkley: University of California Press.

Rudlin, John (1986) *Jacques Copeau*, Cambridge: Cambridge University Press.

Sklar, Deidre (1985) "Etienne Decroux's Promethean Mime," *The Drama Review* 29(4): T108.

Sklar, Deidre, and Cohen-Cruz, Jan (1993) "Chez Decroux circa 1968," *Words on Decroux*, Claremont, CA: Mime Journal.

Soum, Corinne (1999) "A Little History of a Great Transmission or Simplon's Tunnel," *Transmission*, Claremont, CA: Mime Journal.

Souriau, Paul (1983) *The Aesthetics of Movement*, trans. and ed. Manon Souriau, Amherst: The University of Massachusetts Press.

Thody, Philip (1977) *Roland Barthes: A Conservative Estimate*, Chicago, IL: University of Chicago Press.

—— (1983) *Roland Barthes: A Conservative Estimate*, Chicago, IL: University of Chicago Press.

White, Hayden (1987) *The Content of the Form*, Baltimore, MD: The Johns Hopkins University Press.

Wylie, Kathryn (1993) "The Body Politic of Corporeal Mime," *Words on Decroux*, Claremont, CA: Mime Journal.

INDEX

Artaud, Antonin 11, 86

Barba, Eugenio 3, 6, 23, 26–7, 62, 78, 102
Barrault, Jean-Louis 10–11, 12, 14, 16, 51, 66
Baty, Gaston 9, 11, 59
Bellugue, Paul 25
Bing, Suzanne 6, 8, 26, 43, 45
Bogart, Anne 27

Carpentier, Georges 3, 53–4
Children of Paradise 10, 12–13
Copeau, Jacques 6–9, 11, 15–16, 19, 23, 26, 42–8, 50, 51, 54–5, 58, 59, 68
Corporeal Mime 1, 3, 6, 11, 13, 14, 15, 17, 19, 25, 26, 32, 34, 35–7, 39, 40, 42, 43, 44, 45, 46, 51, 52, 53, 54–5, 56, 57, 58, 60, 62, 63–5, 66, 68, 69, 70, 75, 76, 81–3, 85, 106, 113
Craig, Edward Gordon 6, 7, 14, 17, 40, 42, 51–3, 56
cubism 23, 81, 94, 126

Deburau, Charles xiii, 3, 5
Deburau, Jean-Gaspard 10, 12, 13

Decroux, Maximilien 17, 18, 111
Decroux, Suzanne (Lodieu) 9–10, 18, 136
Delsarte, François 70, 120
Dorcy, Jean 14, 15, 17, 42, 46, 48, 49–50
Dullin, Charles 6, 9, 10, 11, 42, 48
dynamo-rhythm 32, 58–60, 81–3, 84, 93, 98, 116

Flash, Marise xiv, 106, 107–10

Grotowski, Jerzy 26, 27–31, 32, 34, 36, 37, 38, 55, 59
Guyon, Eliane 13, 14, 16

Hébert, Lt. Georges 7, 8, 21, 59

improvisation 7–8, 21–2, 44–5, 51, 59, 68, 70, 74, 85, 107, 114, 134

Jouvet, Louis 6, 9, 11, 42

Lecoq, Jacques 21, 46, 73, 90

Marceau, Marcel 13–14, 23, 77
Marey, Etienne-Jules 64

Mask 3, 7, 16, 22, 24, 43–5, 47–51, 57, 69, 71, 78, 84, 96–7, 111
Meyerhold, Vsevolod 23, 68, 69, 84

Noh 6, 26–7, 38, 43, 45–6, 50, 113

pantomime 1, 3, 10, 12–14, 17, 23, 36, 42, 44, 54, 57, 63, 64, 66, 81, 84, 138
Pronko, Leonard 26

Shawn, Ted 66, 120
Soum, Corinne xiii, xiv, 35, 74–5, 86, 88, 105, 106
Stanislavsky, Konstantin 23, 86

Wasson, Steven xiii, xiv, 35, 88, 105, 106

Zeami, Motokiyo 26, 37, 38

Related titles from Routledge

Theatre Histories:
An Introduction

Edited by Philip B. Zarrilli, Bruce McConahie, Gary Jay Williams and Carol Fisher Sorgenfrei

'This book will significantly change theatre education'
Janelle Reinelt, *University of California, Irvine*

Theatre Histories: An Introduction is a radically new way of looking at both the way history is written and the way we understand performance.

The authors provide beginning students and teachers with a clear, exciting journey through centuries of Eurpoean, North the South American, African and Asian forms of theatre and performance.

Challenging the standard format of one-volume theatre history texts, they help the reader think critically about this vibrant field through fascinating yet plain-speaking essays and case studies.

Among the topics covered are:

- representation and human expression
- interpretation and critical approaches
- historical method and sources
- communication technologies
- colonization
- oral and literate cultures
- popular, sacred and elite forms of performance.

Keeping performance and culture very much centre stage, *Theatre Histories: An Introduction* is compatible with standard play anthologies, full of insightful pedagogical apparatus, and comes accompanied by web site resources.

ISBN Hb: 978–0–415–22727–8
ISBN Pb: 978–0–415–22728–5

Available at all good bookshops
For ordering and futher information please visit:
www.routledge.com

Related titles from Routledge

The Routledge Companion to Theatre and Performance

Edited by Paul Allain and Jen Harvie

What is theatre? What is performance? What are their connections and differences? What events, people, practices and ideas have shaped theatre and performance in the twentieth century, and, importantly, where are they heading next?

Proposing answers to these big questions, *The Routledge Companion to Theatre and Performance* provides an informative and engaging introduction to the significant people, events, concepts and practices that have defined the complementary fields of theatre and performance studies.

Including over 120 entries in three easy-to-use, alphabetical sections, this fascinating text presents a wide range of individuals and topics, from performance artist Marina Abramovic, to directors Vsevolod Meyerhold and Robert Wilson, The Living Theatre's *Paradise Now*, *the haka*, multimedia performance, political protest and visual theatre.

With each entry containing crucial historical and contextual information, extensive cross-referencing, detailed analysis, and an annotated bibliography, *The Routledge Companion to Theatre and Performance* is undoubtedly a perfect reference guide for the keen student and passionate theatre-goer alike.

ISBN Hb: 978–0–415–25720–6
ISBN Pb: 978–0–415–25721–3

Available at all good bookshops
For ordering and further information please visit:
www.routledge.com

Related titles from Routledge

Performance Studies: An Introduction
2nd Edition
Richard Schechner

Praise for the first edition:
'An appropriately broad-ranging, challenging, and provocative
introduction, equally important for practicing artists as for students and
scholars of the performing arts.'

- Phillip Zarrilli, *University of Exeter*

Fully revised and updated in light of recent world events, this important
new edition of a key introductory textbook by a prime mover in the field
provides a lively and accessible overview of the full range of performance.

Performance Studies includes discussion of the performing arts and popular
entertainments, rituals, play and games as well as the performances of
every day life. Supporting examples and ideas are drawn from the
performing arts, anthropology, post-structuralism, ritual theory, ethology,
philosophy and aesthetics.

The text has been fully revised, with input from leading teachers and trialled
with students. User-friendly, with a special text design, it also includes:

- new examples, biographies, source material and photographs
- numerous extracts from primary sources giving alternative voices
  and viewpoints
- biographies of key thinkers
- activities to stimulate fieldwork, classroom exercises and discussion
- key readings for each chapter
- twenty line drawings and 202 photographs drawn from private and
  public collections around the world.

For undergraduates at all levels and beginning graduate students in performance studies, theatre, performing arts and cultural studies, this is the
must-have book in the field.

Hb: 978–0–415–37245–9
Pb: 978–0–415–37246–6

Available at all good bookshops
For ordering and further information please visit:
www.routledge.com